20 Pencil People Patterns for Carvers

Al Streetman

4880 Lower Valley Road, Atglen, PA 19310 USA

Dedication

To my Dad, without whose help I would not have the knowledge, skills, or equipment to photograph my books and continue to be able to turn ideas into reality.

Acknowledgments

The following people helped make this book possible. I thank you all.

Marilynn Jones: For your continued word-processing support, both in data entry, and especially in data retrieval.

Jody Garrett, Woodcraft Supply Corp.: For all the help you give to us "starving artists," and for providing us with various carving tool samples for evaluation and consideration.

Delta Technical Coatings, Inc.: The paint samples were excellent and satisfactory in all respects.

Woodcraft Supply Corp.; Parkersburg, West Virginia: Excellent carving tools and supplies.

Royal Brush Mfg.,Inc.: Excellent quality paintbrushes at an affordable price.

Copyright © 1997 by Al Streetman
Library of Congress Catalog Card Number: 97-80113

Designed by Laurie A. Smucker

ISBN: 0-7643-0034-2
Printed in China
1 2 3 4

Published by Schiffer Publishing Ltd.
4880 Lower Valley Road
Atglen, PA 19310
Phone: (610) 593-1777; Fax: (610) 593-2002
E-mail: Schifferbk@aol.com

Please write for a free catalog.
This book may be purchased from the publisher.
Please include $3.95 for shipping.

Try your bookstore first.

We are interested in hearing from authors
with book ideas on related subjects.

Contents

Introduction

For those of you who have accumulated piles of long, narrow wood scraps as a result of sawing other patterns out, this book may be of help. I kept looking at my pile of scraps (I never throw good wood away), and I said to myself, "There must be a use for these pieces of skinny wood!" Pencil people are the result of my soul-searching. They will give good caricature-carving practice, but because the features are exaggerated in the vertical plane, you have a bit more freedom so far as having to be "anatomically correct" in all senses of the word.

I have attempted to give you a variety of patterns and I hope these will be enough to spur your imagination and help you visualize other potential pencil people in your private pile of wood scraps.

In the carving chapter, I will be sharing some of my tricks and secrets regarding head, hand, and body carving. I hope the methods I use and teach will give you some new insight into character carving techniques and will make carving easier and more fun for you.

Some of you may observe that my carving project is not as complex or detailed as you might carve it. There is a method to my madness. I have tried to design a project that yields a nice result, yet isn't too complex or involved for a beginning woodcarver to accomplish. I want to reach as many woodcarvers as possible, and share the joy of carving with them. As beginners gain more experience, they can add additional details as desired.

Except for the actual carving project, I have not included specific carving instructions for each pattern. I have found that each carver has his or her own style and each has a preference for which tool to use in a particular area, or to achieve a particular effect.

Rather than giving vague instructions such as "use a small gouge," I have listed the particular size gouge I used in the different steps of the carving project. This is more for the benefit of the beginning carver than the more experienced ones. If you don't have these particular sizes of gouges or tools, use something similar. The world won't come to a crashing end if you don't use the same exact tools I used.

The patterns in this book include approximate dimensions for the side and front views, if you desire to carve them to the same size as I originally designed them.

If you desire a larger or smaller version, simply enlarge or shrink the pattern on a photocopying machine. You may also want to use the photocopying machine to make several sizes of the hand template. This way you will be sure to have a hand outline that is the proper size for the figure you carve.

You will notice that the patterns contain several drawings: a side and front profile with dimensions, which is the pattern you will use to saw out the body blank; a head pattern, and in some instances an accessory, depending on the pattern you are going to carve. The numbers on the arms of the patterns correspond to numbers on the hand template and are the suggested hands to use for that pattern. If you would rather use different hands, feel free to do so. This will allow you to achieve many different looks from just a few patterns.

Before you begin the actual carving project, I *highly recommend* that you read through the entire book at least once. You may notice that a detail that was not completely clear to you in the carving section may become *very clear* in the painting section. Often the details show up much better once the wood has been given some life with a coat of paint. Remember, if we carve it in the first part of the book, we'll paint it later, so you have at least two sections of the book for a reference. Many of these characters will also show up in the gallery and study model section, so that will give you a third source for a reference.

I use basswood whenever possible, but any soft wood such as jelutong, clear spruce, or sugar/white pine will work equally well. If possible, use a bandsaw with a 1/8" blade to cut out the side and front profiles. The bandsaw will allow you to release the rough version of the figure from the block of wood faster than trying to use a coping saw or other means to cut out the pattern.

General Notes

1. Trace the head, body, and accessory pattern, or make a copy of it on a photocopying machine. Glue the pattern you copied or traced onto some heavy paper such as poster paper or a manila file folder. When the glue is dry, cut out the pattern. This method will prevent you from ruining the master patterns in your book. Also, make a copy of the hand template, glue it to some heavy paper, and cut it out. You can use it on various carving projects when it is time to make the hands and fit them to the body.

2. Lay your pattern on the wood, trace the outline of it, and saw it out. The arrows shown on the patterns, with a "G" superimposed over them, indicate the recommended grain direction of the wood to obtain best results and easiest carving.

3. You should now have a rough blank ready to be carved.

4. Use your own techniques and style to bring the carving to the finished stage.

5. You will notice that some of the patterns to be used for sawing out the body do not show hands attached. The numbers on the arms indicate the recommended hand for that pattern. This is where you will use the hand template. This method allows you to carve the body then decide on the size and style of hands you want to use for that carving. Many times the type of hands will be determined by what accessories you are going to include with the carving. If you carve the hands separately from the body, you can orient them to take advantage of the wood grain when you saw them out. This will allow you endless variations of hand positions, so you can give more life to your carvings. Also, if you are creating an extreme caricature, you can use a larger than normal hand pattern to add more humor to the carving.

6. We are also going to carve the head separately from the main body in the carving project. This gives you several advantages: (a) if you make a mistake on the head or body, the other part won't be ruined ; (b) you can assemble the head to the body looking straight ahead or you can turn it to one side (turning the head to one side will give more "life" to your carvings); (c) You can "mix and match" different heads with different bodies, therefore gaining more variations from a given number of patterns.

7. If you carve the pistols, rifles, or other accessories as separate pieces you can orient them to get maximum strength from the grain direction, and this also gives you more flexibility in positioning them on the body, or in the hands.

Project Carving Tools

For those of you who may want to duplicate the cuts I made using the same tools as I used, I have listed below the tools used in the carving project.

1/8" V gouge
1/4" V gouge
2-millimeter, #11 U gouge
8-millimeter #2 Flat gouge
3-millimeter #11 U gouge
Fixed blade (Bütz) carving and detail knives

For those of you who are not familiar with the type of cuts different gouges make, or how large the cut is for a specific size of gouge, I have included a "Gouge Reference Chart" at the end of the book. If you want to use a different gouge other than one which I used, this chart will be helpful in determining what type of gouge you might want to try.

General Tips
Eyes

QUILT PIN METHOD: I often use various sizes of plastic-head quilting pins to make eyes. Mark where you want the eyes to be on the finished carving. Using a drill and a bit that is slightly larger than the pinhead you are going to use, make a hole for each eye.

Using wire cutters, snip off the pinhead, leaving about 1/4" of the pin attached to the head.

Insert the pinhead into the eye socket, with the pin end going in first. Use a nail set to seat the head into the hole until only a small orb protrudes. This gives a fairly realistic eye without causing too much effort on your part. For extra detail, remove a triangular-shaped piece of wood from the sides of the pinhead. This will make a very realistic eye when it is painted.

PUNCH METHOD: A second easy way to create eyes is to use carver's eye punches. Select the size eye punch you want to use, based on the size of the eye sockets you have made. Push the eye punch against the socket firmly and rotate it. After making both eyes, remove triangular-shaped pieces of wood from the corners to give more detail. Use your knife, if necessary, to smooth and round off the eyeball.

FOOTBALL METHOD: A more realistic way to make eyes is to, first of all, carve the eye sockets so that about a 90-degree angle is formed. Lightly sketch in a football-shaped eye in each socket so that the top half of the football is on the upper half of the socket and the lower half of the football is on the lower half of the socket. When you sketch in the footballs, make the outside ends lower than the inside ends. Using the tip of your knife, score the football outline to a depth of about 1/16". Now use the tip of your knife to remove triangular-shaped pieces of wood from the left and right corner of each eye. This will leave a small section of wood inside each football, which will be the eyeball. Use your knife to round off and smooth the eyeball. You can vary the way you remove the triangular-shaped corners if you want the eyes to be looking more to one side rather than straight ahead.

MOUND METHOD: The most realistic way to make eyes is to first rough carve the nose so it stands out from the face. Next, sketch a circle or oval on each side of the nose to represent where the eye mounds will be located. Using a smaller "V" gouge such as a 1/8" size, or your knife tip, go around the circles or ovals so the mounds will be defined, and separated from the face area. Use your knife to round the sharp edges of the mounds and the face area around the mounds.

Divide the mounds into thirds by sketching two curved horizontal lines across each one, making sure that the lines join at each corner of the mound.(Look at your own eyes in a mirror to see what I mean here). Using your knife tip, score each horizontal line about 1/16" deep. Working from the center of the eye mound, use your knife tip to shave **upward** toward the top horizontal line, and **downward** toward the bottom horizontal line. This will make the eyelids stand out from the eyeball area. Finally, remove small triangular pieces of wood from each corner of the eye, so the eyeball will be rounded from left to right, as well as top to bottom.

Changing the size and shape of the mounds, and the spacing between the horizontal lines, will allow you to achieve many effects and expressions on your carvings.

One last thing concerning eyes: Don't get upset if you discover that you have carved one eye smaller or at a different angle than the other eye. This "accident" may work to your advantage. It will lend an interesting variation to the carving, and no one has to know you didn't do it that way on purpose!!

Buying Wood

When buying wood, whether it be basswood, spruce, or some other type, try to pick the lightest pieces. They tend to have less fat and sap in them so they are easier to carve.

On Rifles

If making a rifle for your carving, it is easier and more realistic if you make the barrel separate from the stock. The best material for the barrel is 1/16" aluminum tubing which can be purchased at any hobby or hardware store. To cut it to length, simply roll it lightly back and forth under your knife blade. It is a soft metal and won't hurt your knife edge. After carving the woodstock, a small amount of cement such as Ambroid or DuPont will hold the barrel firmly in place. An alternate method for the barrel is to use a section of 1/8" wood dowel, glued in place and painted silver.

Wrinkles

An easy way to help determine where you want to place some wrinkles and folds in the arms, torso, and legs is to observe and note where the wood grain changes direction as you are carving. Usually in the crook of an elbow or behind the knees, you will notice that wood "fuzzies" try to appear, no matter how carefully you carve or how sharp your knife is. That is because the wood grain direction is changing and, in one direction or the other, you are trying to carve against the grain, thus the "fuzzies" appear. These spots are perfect candidates for wrinkles and folds, made with a large "V" tool or by cutting wedges out with your knife. As a beginning carver, if you do nothing more than add a few cuts in these areas, you will be amazed at the difference in the way the carving looks. With experience, you will start noticing other places to add wrinkles and folds.

Photocopying

For those of you who haven't had much practice enlarging or reducing patterns, or being able to calculate how much enlargement or reduction you need to select on the photocopying machine, here are some general guidelines:

Let's say you have a pattern that shows a side profile requiring 2" thick wood, and you want to make the pattern larger so it will fit on 3" thick wood. Use the following formula to calculate what percentage enlargement to select on the copier:

[New Dimension Desired ÷ Present Dimension] x 100 = percent to select on copier machine. Using our example, this would work out as follows: [3" ÷ 2"] x 100 = 150 percent.

Going the other way, let's say you have a pattern that shows a 2" side profile, and you want to reduce it down so it will fit on a piece of 1-3/4" thick wood. Using the same formula, it works out as follows:

[1.75" ÷ 2"] x 100 = 87.5 percent.

If the machine you are using won't cut large enough or small enough to get the job done on the first try, additional steps may be required. Go ahead and make your first copy using the largest enlargement or reduction setting you can select. Measure the new dimensions on your copy, (which will now be your *present dimension*), then use the same formula as before to calculate how much additional enlargement or reduction is needed to get the pattern to the size you desired it to be.

Hands

When making separate hands that are going to be holding some object, such as a rifle, it is easiest if you first cut out the top profile of the hand, drill a hole large enough for the object to fit through, then saw out the side profile of the hand. This procedure will help prevent the hand from splitting when you drill it.

Spread 'Em

On the patterns where the legs are together rather than spread apart, you may want to separate them slightly by sawing on a line from the bottom of the feet, up to where the crotch would be. You can do this with your bandsaw or a coping saw. This line will help you keep the legs symmetrical and centered on the body.

Keeping Your Head On

When drilling a hole in the body for the neck and head, you may wish to do so before you saw the body from the wood. First, transfer the side and front pattern profiles to the wood. Next, locate the center of the body on both profiles. Mark this location and drill down into the wood. Use a drill bit that is the proper size for the neck you carved and go deep enough into the block so you will have a neck hole after the body is sawed loose from the block. This method prevents the wood from splitting as you drill, especially in instances where you have a slim body profile.

Rounding Your Edges

If you are not familiar with the technique of "rounding," it is merely the process of continuously removing sharp edges until a square section of wood becomes round, or as round as you want it to be. For practice, cut a 1" x 1" x 3" long section of wood. Use your knife to remove the four sharp edges, and you will now have an eight-sided section of wood, 3" long. Use your knife to remove the new sharp edges, and you will see that the section of wood is rapidly approaching a round, or cylindrical shape. When bringing arms, legs, and body sections to a rounded shape, this is the technique that will get you there. Some people prefer to get a section of their carving almost perfectly round, while others like to leave the areas less rounded, so the knife cuts and facets may be seen. I personally like the latter effect, because it makes the carving look more like a carving and less like a molded product.

Tips for Cowboys

• I normally use the same thickness of wood for the head as I use for the body. This provides plenty of wood for a big, floppy hat brim.

• If you want your cowboy to have a "scruffy" look rather than a well-manicured look, you may want to add some beard stubble to the cheek, chin, and neck areas. This may be done by pricking small pieces of wood loose using a very tiny "V" gouge (such as a 1/8" "V" gouge), or by making small indentations in the wood using the sharpened tip of a small finishing nail or electric engraving tool. An alternate method, if you prefer, is to add the stubble detail using a burning device such as a Hot Tool, Detail Master, etc.

After painting the flesh and hair color, very lightly dry-brush a small amount of black onto the beard stubble area, to give that five-o'clock shadow look. If you have painted the hair gray or white to depict an old, grizzly cowboy, you may want to dry-brush small amounts of black and gray onto the beard stubble area.

• If you want your cowboy to have a dusty, trail-worn appearance, *lightly* dry-brush *small* amounts of gray or white paint all over the carving. This will help remove the "new" look from his clothing and accessories.

• An easy way to make "rope" is to use heavy cotton twine. Cut a section of twine, soak it in a thinned-down solution of brown stain or paint, and let it dry. After it is dry, you can position it in the character's hands, loop it around his head, or position it as you desire.

• To make "barbed-wire" fast and easy, obtain a roll of small-gauge wire from the hardware store. Cut a section of wire about 6 feet in length, and fold it in half. Hook the loop end around a nail and clamp the nail in a vise. Insert the two loose ends in an electric drill, chuck them securely, and slowly activate the drill so the wire twists tightly. Remove the ends from the drill and secure them so that the wire remains stretched out and firm. Using small sections of wire, wrap each section around the main wire several times, to form the "barbs." Space the barbs about 3/8" apart on the main wire.

• The most realistic fence posts can be achieved by using small twigs, which have a natural weathered look. If you are unable to obtain twigs, small wooden dowels may be substituted.

• Wire reels for wrapping barbed-wire around may be constructed using sections of wooden dowel as the hub and thin sections of scrap wood as the cross-pieces on the ends.

• To give coffee pots, cups, and plates that old fashioned "enameled" look, paint them with a base coat of white. After the base coat is dry, use a piece of old sponge, and *lightly* dab blue or black over the white.

• Many times, you can find plates, cups, coffee pots, and other accessories which are the right size for your project at stores which carry doll and doll-house supplies.

Tips for Leprechauns

• An easy way to make gold "coins" for your leprechauns is to use various sizes of wooden dowels. Slice them thin with a band saw, coping saw, or other means, paint them gold, and place them as desired around the carving.

• If you want to have pots of gold with your leprechaun, but don't want to try carving them, wooden candle cups make excellent pots. These are available at various craft and hobby stores and supply houses and come in many different sizes. Fill the bottom part with paper, paint the whole thing black, then put some of your wooden coins in the top part. You can make a realistic pot of gold quickly by using this method. A scrap piece of wire makes an excellent handle for the pots.

Tips for Uncle Sam

• An easy way to make stars is to take a stylus or toothpick and put a dot of white paint where you want the star to be. Starting inside the dot, while the paint is still wet, drag the tip of the stylus or toothpick toward the edge and out to make a line. Do this for all five points of the star. The bigger you make the dot of paint to begin with, and the further you drag each line outside of the dot, the bigger the star will be.

• Firecrackers are made by sawing a wooden dowel to the desired length, then drilling a 1/16" hole in one end. Insert a small-gauge piece of wire into the hole to be the fuse.

• Make rockets in the same manner as firecrackers, but carve a point on the opposite end from the fuse. Use a small stick such as a toothpick to make the "tail" stick on the rocket.

Tips for Santas

• For realistic fur, I use a product made by Delta Technical Coatings, Inc. called "Decorative Snow." This is a white, grainy acrylic mixture that you apply with a small flat brush. After it is dry and painted, it gives a very good fur look.

• If you don't want to try carving the "pom-pom" ball on Santa's hat, you can make one the easy way by using unpainted wooden beads which can be obtained at most craft stores. Buy various sizes, then use one which best fits the hat, after the head and hat are carved. Carve a flat spot on the hat, and glue the bead to it. If the bead has a hole in it, fill the hole with wood filler after the glue dries. This method is the most realistic one I have found for making the pom-poms.

Painting Suggestions

I have listed colors produced by Delta Technical Coatings, Inc. and their identification numbers, which I have found to be suitable for painting the carving project and all my other carvings. I have used these colors and the results were excellent. I hope this will help minimize your confusion when trying to sort through the maze of paint brands and colors at your hobby or craft store. The best paintbrushes I have found for the money are made by the Royal Brush Mfg. Company. They come in a wide assortment of sizes and shapes, are durable, and most important are affordable. In general, here are the ones I use and recommend for painting your carvings:

• Royal Golden Taklon series 250 Round, Size 0 and 00, for details such as eyes and other small areas.

• Royal Golden Taklon Series 170 Cat's Tongue, Size 2 and 4 for large areas.

• Royal Golden Taklon Series 150 Short Shader, Size 2 and 4, for blending colors. (For example, when blending a "blush" color into the flesh color on faces, hands, etc.)

You may have heard and read this a million times, but when painting your carvings, keep the word THIN in mind. What you want to do is stain the wood to give it some color and life, but you don't want the paint so thick that it covers up the beauty of the wood.

NOTE: When painting the head and hands, I generally use a slightly thicker mixture of paint than I use on the rest of the carving. I want the face to be a bit more intense than the rest of the carving, since the head and face are what sets most of the mood for the carving.

Carving Project Colors

Fleshtone #2019	White #2505
Blue Heaven #2037	Black #2506
Dark Brown #2053	Quaker Grey #2057
Crimson #2076	Navy Blue #2089
Kim Gold #2602	Antique White #2001
Silver #2603	Trail Tan #2435
Walnut #2024	Burnt Sienna #2030
Ocean Reef Blue #2074	Brown Iron Oxide #2023
Bright Yellow #2027	Vibrant Green #2007
Cadet Grey #2426	

Santa

White #2505 (Beards, eyebrows, eyes,)
Antique White #2001 (Fur)
Black #2506 (Boots, belts, mittens, dot in eyes)
Fleshtone #2019 (Face,hands)

Sweetheart Blush #2130 (For blending on face and nose areas, to give a weatherbeaten look)
Blue Heaven #2037 (Light blue for dot in eyes)
Crimson #2076 (Coats)
Cardinal Red #2077 (Coats)
Bright Red #2503 (Stripes on candy canes)
Territorial Beige #2425 (Bags)
Pigskin #2093 (Boots)\

Cowboy

White #2505	Sandstone #2402
Antique White #2001	Black #2506
Fleshtone #2019	Burnt Sienna #2030
Burnt Umber #2025	Walnut #2024
Blue Heaven #2037	Crocus Yellow #2459
Denim Blue #2477	Crimson #2076
Navy Blue #2089	Quaker Grey #2057
Silver #2603	Red Iron Oxide #2020
Territorial Beige #2425	Cadet Gray #2426
Autumn Brown #2055	GP Purple #2091
Pigskin #2093	Trail Tan #2435
Palomino Tan #2108	Lilac Dusk #2403
Persimmon #2480	

FACE, EARS, NECK AND HANDS: Fleshtone.

EYES: White base. Then paint a dot of Blue Heaven in the center, corner or top of eye. Next, paint a smaller dot of black in the blue dot. Finally, use a toothpick and put a white highlight on the edge of the black dot.

HAIR, MUSTACHE AND EYEBROWS: White, black, brown or a color of your choice.

HATS: Black, Pigskin, Trail Tan, Cadet Gray, Quaker Gray, Burnt Umber, or a color of your choice. If a hatband was also carved, paint it a contrasting color to the hat so it will show up.

SHIRTS: Crimson, White, Persimmon, Lilac Dusk, GP Purple, or a color of your choice.

BUTTONS ON SHIRTS: Black, silver, or a color of your choice.

PANTS: Denim Blue, Sandstone, or a color of your choice.

BANDANNAS: Crimson, with Crocus Yellow dots; Navy Blue with white dots; Crocus Yellow with crimson dots, or a color and pattern of your choice.

CIGARETTES: Antique White, with Quaker Gray ash on tip.

BOOTS: Autumn Brown, black, Burnt Umber, Red Iron Oxide, or a color of your choice.

GUNBELTS, HOLSTER, BELTS: Burnt Sienna, black, Red Iron Oxide, or a color of your choice.

BELT BUCKLES: Silver.
PISTOLS: Silver, with walnut hand grips.

Uncle Sam

White #2505 (Hair, eyebrows, eyes, stripes.)
Black #2506 (shoes, dot in eyes, buttons)
Fleshtone #2019 (Face, hands)
Sweetheart Blush #2130 (For blending on face and nose areas)
Blue Heaven #2037 (Light blue for dot in eyes)
Kim Gold #2602 (Buttons on coat)
Naphthol Red Light #2409 (Stripes)
Navy Blue #2089 (Hat, coat)
Antique Gold #2002 (Vest)

Leprechaun

White #2505	Antique White #2001
Black #2506	Fleshtone #2019
Indiana Rose #2018	Rosetta Pink #2430
Burnt Sienna #2030	Tangerine #2043
Spice Tan #2063	Toffee Brown #2086
Pthalo Green #2501	Vibrant Green #2007
Kelly Green #2052	Empire Gold #2412
Brown Iron Oxide #2023	Ocean Reef Blue #2074
Periwinkle Blue	Kim Gold #2602
Silver #2603	Walnut #2024

HAT: Pthalo Green; with Kim Gold Buckle and Burnt Sienna hatband.

FACE, EARS, NECK AND HANDS: Fleshtone, Rosetta Pink, Or Indiana Rose.

Eyes White base. Then paint a dot of Spice Tan in the center, corner, or top of eye. Next, paint a smaller dot of black in the Spice Tan dot. Finally, use a toothpick and put a white highlight on the edge of the black dot.

HAIR, BEARD, AND EYEBROWS: Tangerine.

SHIRTS: Antique White, Periwinkle Blue, or a color of your choice.

VEST: Empire Gold with black buttons.

COAT: Pthalo Green, with Kim Gold buttons.

TROUSERS: Toffee Brown.

STOCKINGS: White, with Periwinkle or Ocean Reef Blue stripes, or a color of your choice.

SHOES: Brown Iron Oxide with Kim Gold buckles.

Gnome

Fleshtone #2019 (Face, ears, neck and hands)
Bright Red #2503 (Hat)
White #2505 (Eyes, highlights in black dot of eye and dry-brushed over Quaker Grey beard)
Blue Heaven #2037 (Large dot in eye)
Black #2506 (Smaller dot in eye)
Blue Danube #2013 (Shirt)
Quaker Grey #2057 (Beard and eyebrows)
Walnut #2024 (Belt)
Silver #2603 (Belt buckle)
Bridgeport Grey #2440 (Boots)

Hillbilly

Fleshtone #2019 (Face, ears, feet, neck and hands)
White #2505 (Eyes, highlights in black dot of eye and dry-brushed over Quaker Grey beard)
Blue Heaven #2037 (Large dot in eye)
Black #2506 (Smaller dot in eye, hat)
Quaker Grey #2057 (Beard and eyebrows)
Walnut #2024 (Rifle stock)
Silver #2603 (Rifle barrel and trigger, buttons on overall straps)
Crimson #2076 (Shirt)
Denim Blue #2477 (Overalls)

Rabbit

Antique White #2001 (Head and feet)
White #2505 (Eyes, highlight in black dot of eye, teeth)
Blue Heaven #2037 (Large dot in eye)
Black #2506 (Smaller dot in eye, nose)
Crimson #2076 (Shirt)
Denim Blue #2477 (Overalls)
Silver #2603 (Buttons on overall straps)

Angel

Fleshtone #2019 (Face)
White #2505 (Eyes, highlights in black dot of eye)
Blue Heaven #2037 (Large dot in eye)
Black #2506 (Smaller dot in eye)
Straw #2078 (Hair and eyebrows)
Antique White #2001 (Wings)
Lavender Lace #2016 (Robe)
14K Gold #2604 (Trim on robe)

Pilgrim

Fleshtone #2019 (Face)
White #2505 (Eyes, highlights in black dot of eye, trim on coat, trim on dress, woman's cap, woman's apron, man's stockings)
Blue Heaven #2037 (Large dot in eye)
Black #2506 (Smaller dot in eye, man's hat, buttons on woman's apron)
Straw #2078 (Woman's hair and eyebrows)
Dark Brown #2053 (Man's hair and eyebrows)
Walnut #2024 (Rifle stock)
Silver #2603 (Rifle barrel and trigger, buckle on hatband, buckle on shoes)
Hammered Iron #2094 (Man's coat and pants, woman's dress)
Brown Iron Oxide #2023 (Man's shoes)

Sea Captain

Fleshtone #2019 (Face, ears and hands)
White #2505 (Eyes, smaller dot in black dot of eyes)
Blue Heaven #2037 (Large dot in eyes)
Black #2506 (Smaller dot in eyes, lower part of hat, main body parts of telescope, left shoe)
Navy Blue #2089 (Coat)
Kim Gold #2602 (Buttons on coat)
Antique White #2001 (Top part of hat)
Silver #2603 (End pieces of telescope, button on peg leg strap)
Walnut #2024 (Peg leg)
Burnt Sienna #2030 (Strap on peg leg)
Cadet Grey #2426 (Beard and eyebrows)
Sandstone #2402 (Trousers)

REMEMBER: These are only a few of the many colors you can use for your carvings. Should you have other color preferences, use them. Don't be afraid to get wild and experiment with all sorts of color combinations. For those of you (like me), who have difficulty trying to decide which colors work well together, most hobby and art supply stores sell inexpensive color wheels which will show you colors that work together and colors that oppose each other. I have listed a few combinations here, for illustrative purposes:

Main Color	Contrast Color
Red	Green
Orange	Blue
Yellow	Violet

A good color wheel will not only show you main and contrast colors, it will also show colors that blend.

Patterns

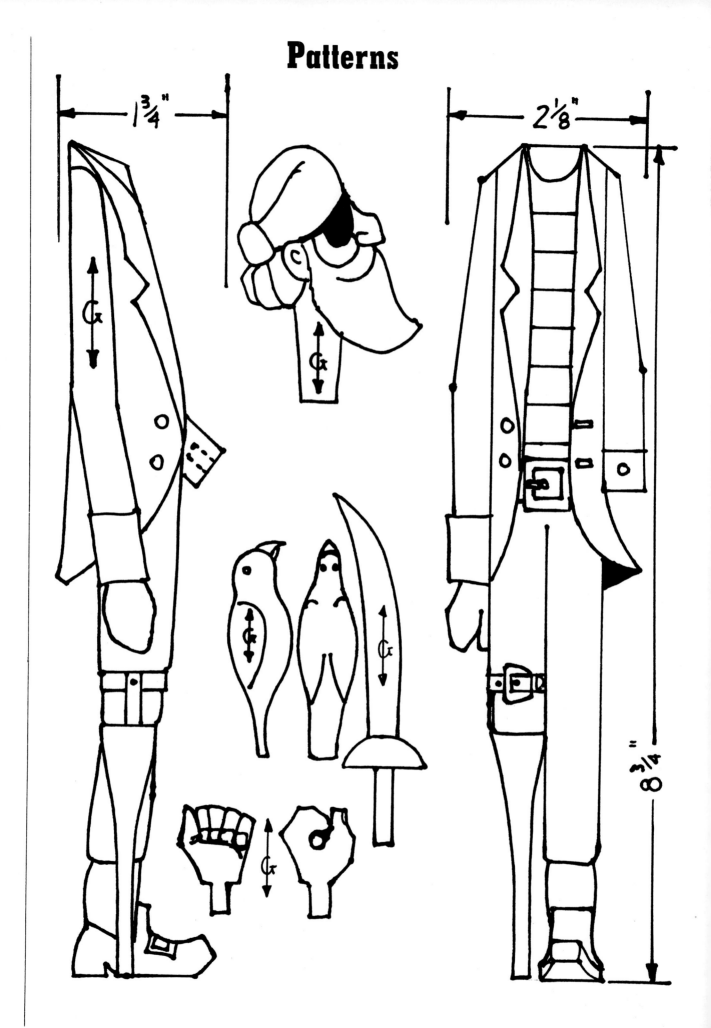

Gnome #1

9⅝"

1¾"

2"

Cowboy #1

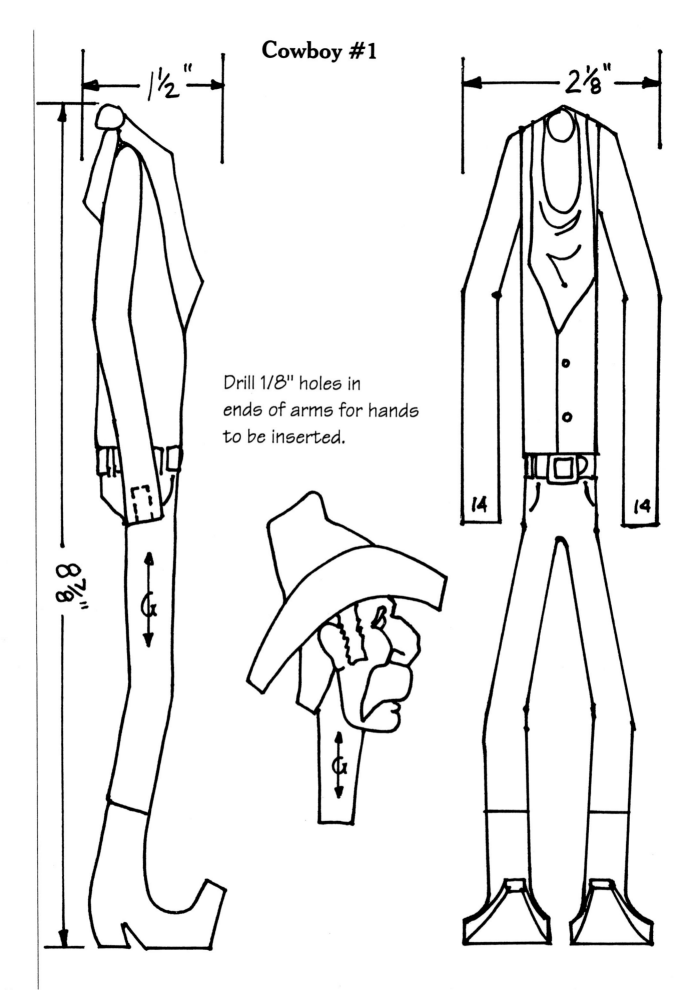

1½"

2⅛"

8⅝"

Drill 1/8" holes in ends of arms for hands to be inserted.

14

14

Uncle Sam #1

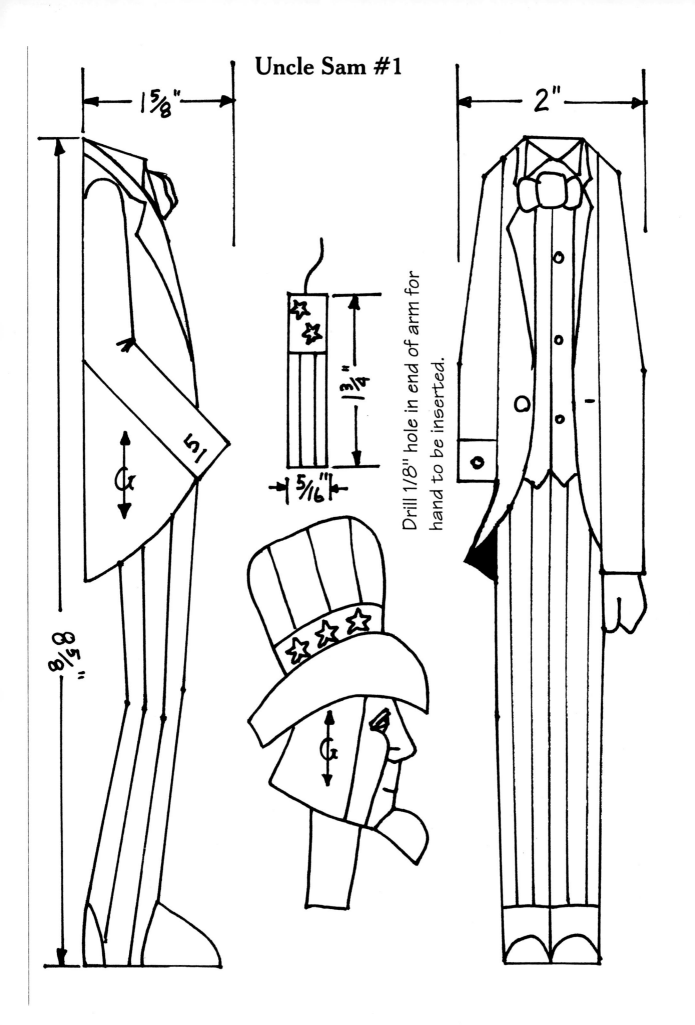

1 5/8"

2"

3/4"

5/16"

8 5/8"

Drill 1/8" hole in end of arm for hand to be inserted.

Firecracker is made from a section of 5/16" wooden dowel. Insert short piece of small wire in end for the fuse.

Santa #1

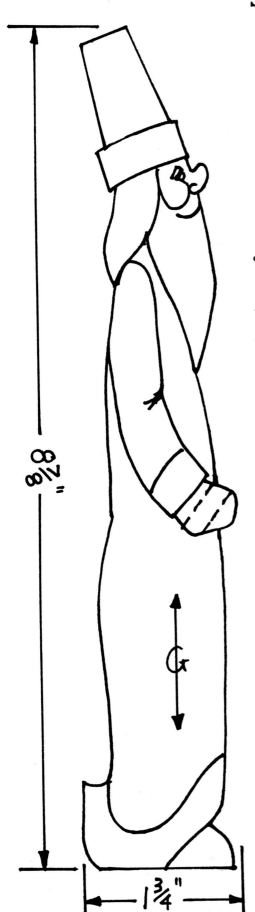

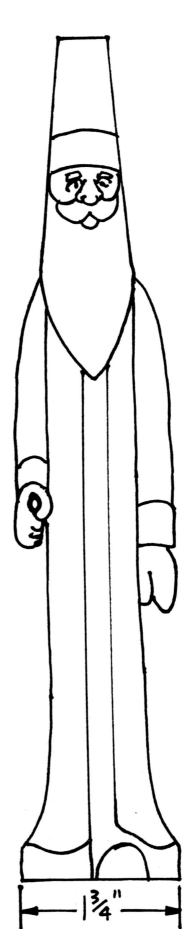

8⅛"

1¾"

1¾"

Drill 3/16" hole through hand at the approximate angle shown for a walking stick. Fashion walking stick from a 3/16" wooden dowel, or small twig.

Hillbilly

1½"

2⅜"

9"

Drill 1/8" hole in end of arm for inserting hand.

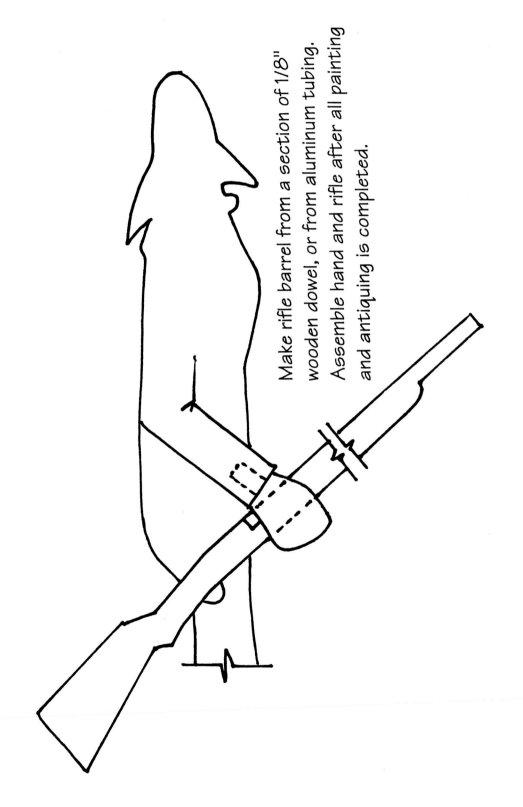

Make rifle barrel from a section of 1/8"
wooden dowel, or from aluminum tubing.
Assemble hand and rifle after all painting
and antiquing is completed.

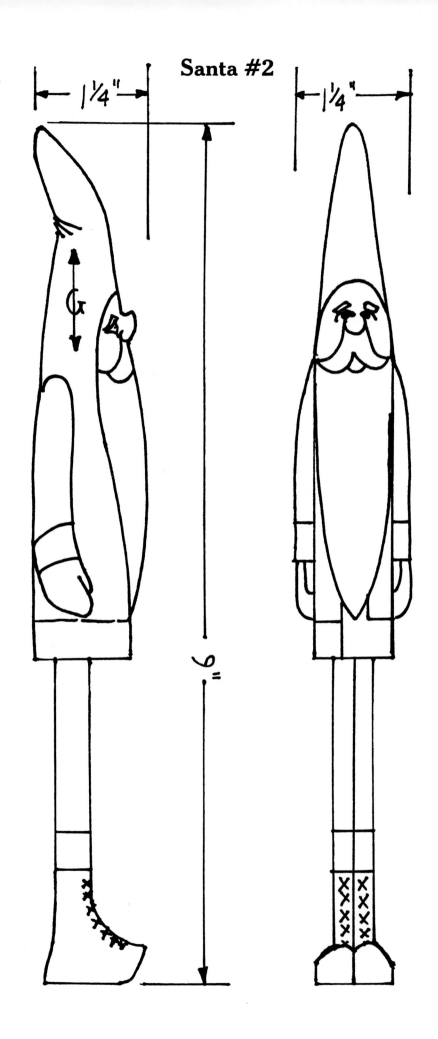

Santa #3

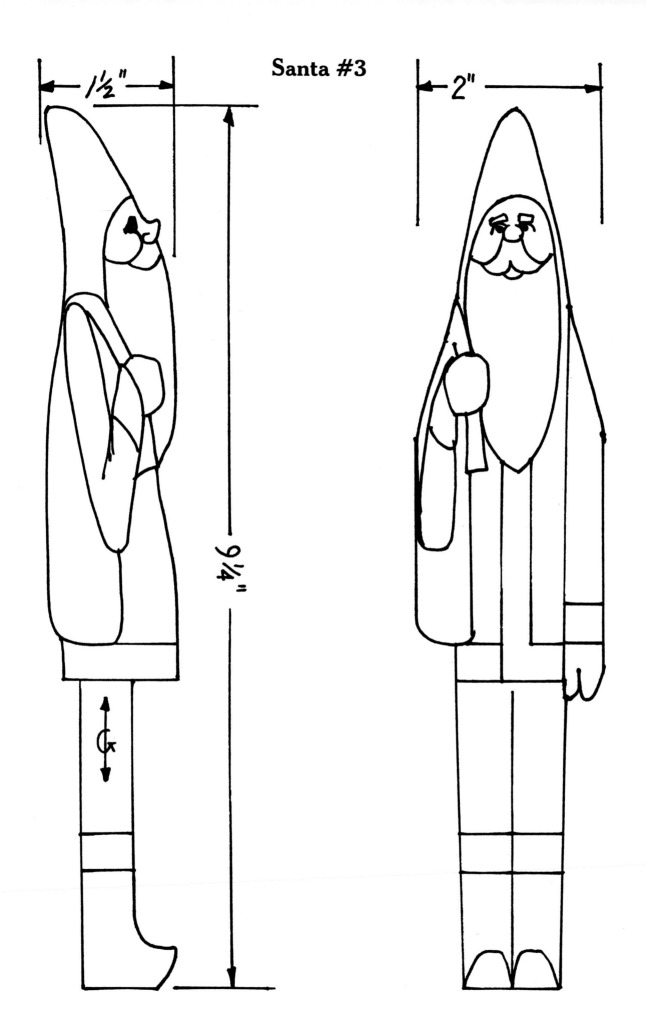

1½"

2"

9¼"

Cowboy #2

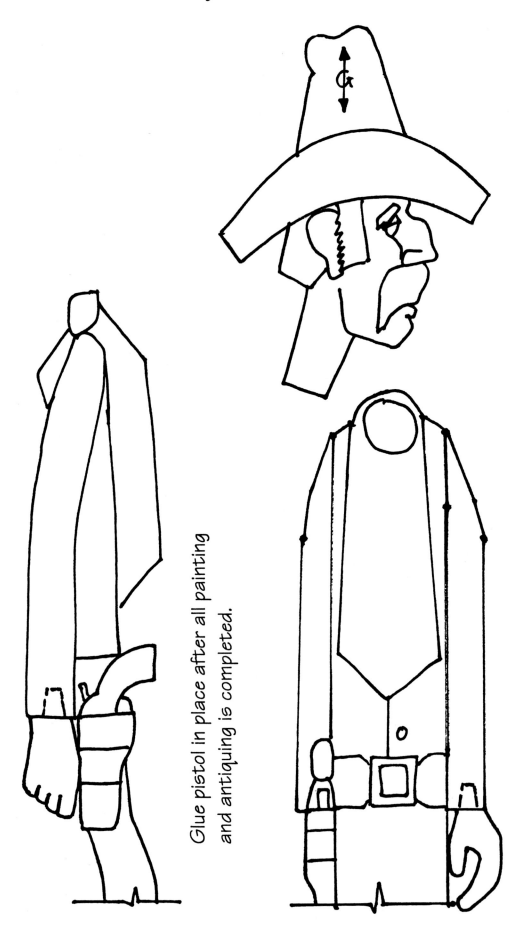

Glue pistol in place after all painting and antiquing is completed.

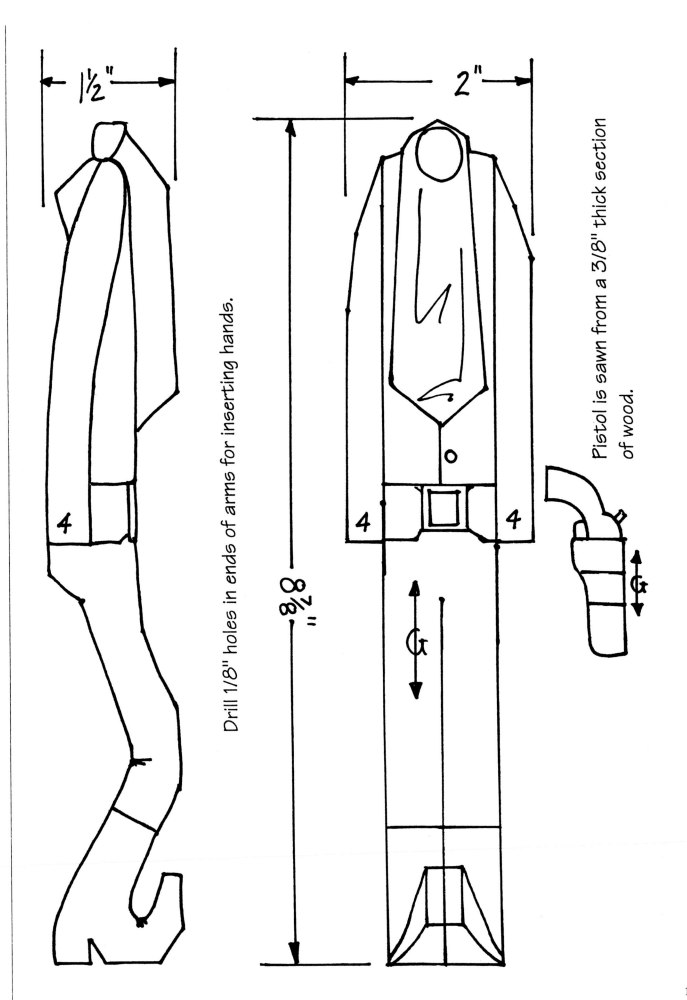

1½"

2"

8⅞"

4

4

4

℄

℄

℄

Drill 1/8" holes in ends of arms for inserting hands.

Pistol is sawn from a 3/8" thick section of wood.

Angel

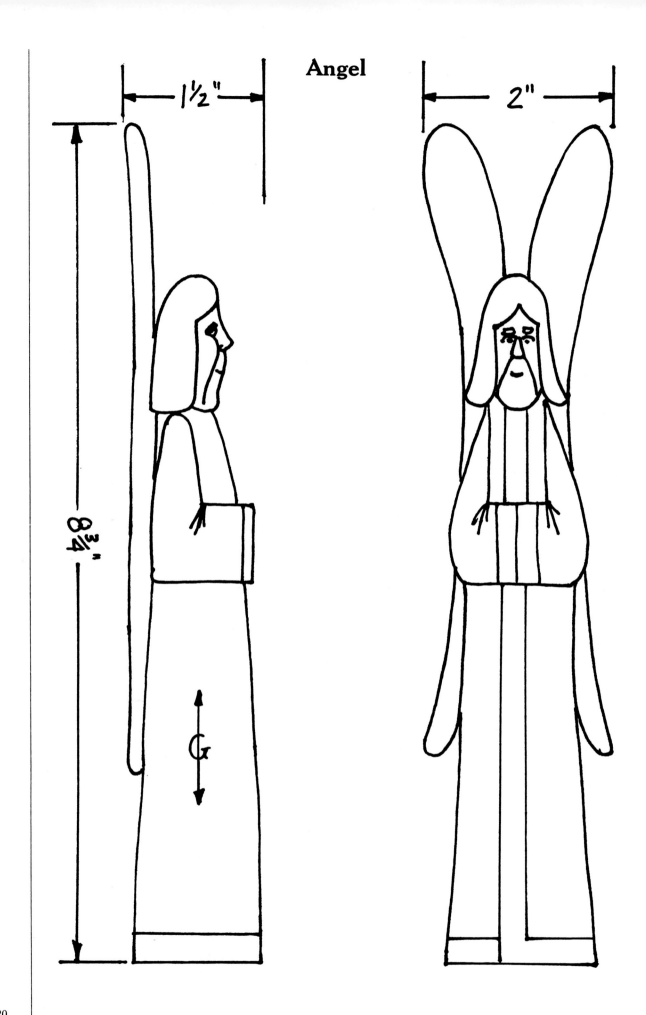

Leprechaun #1

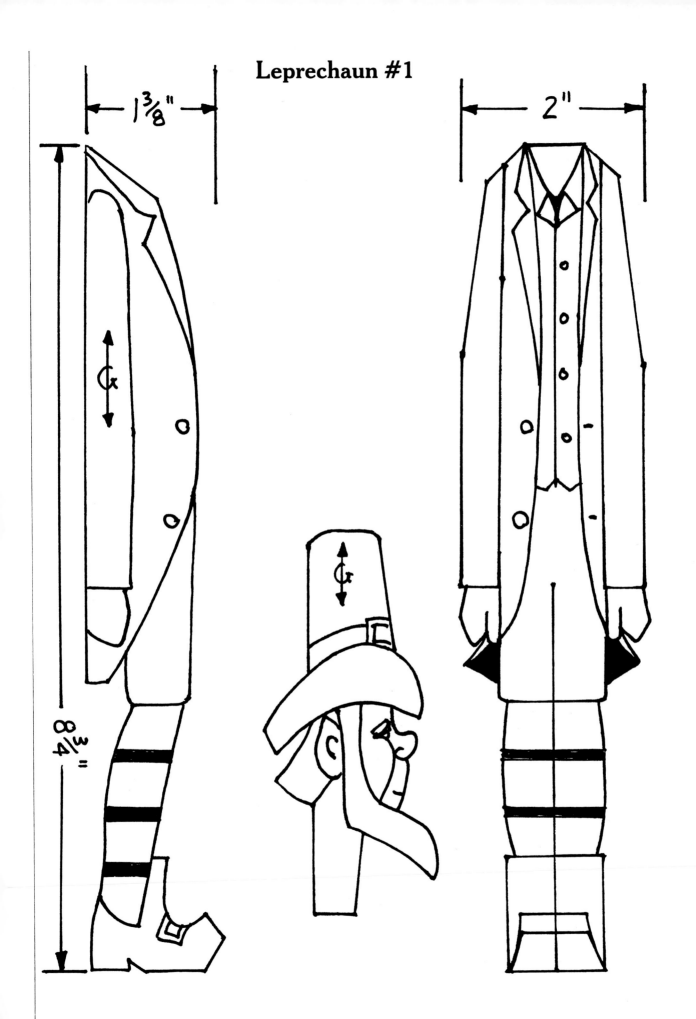

1⅜"

2"

8¾"

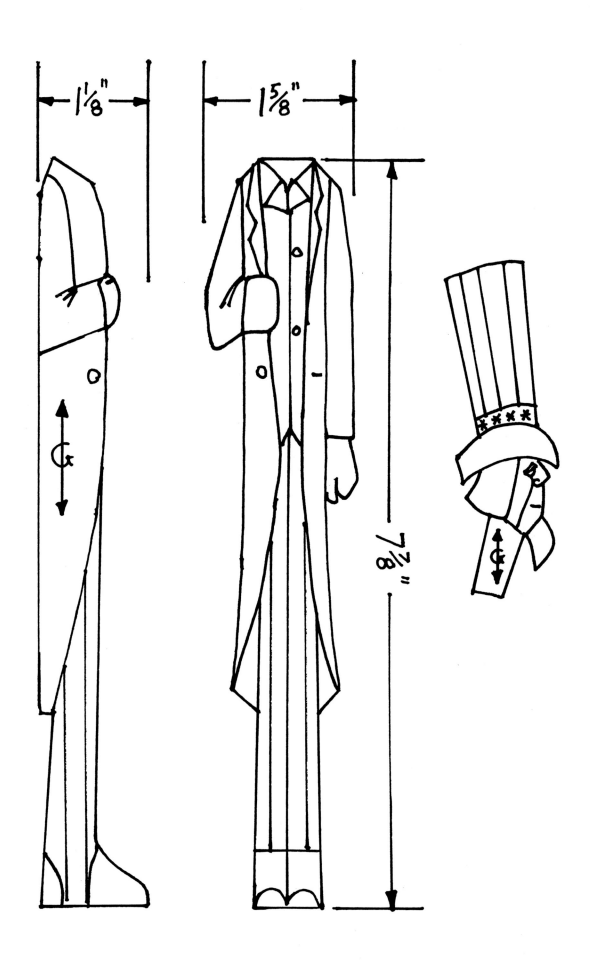

Pilgrim Man

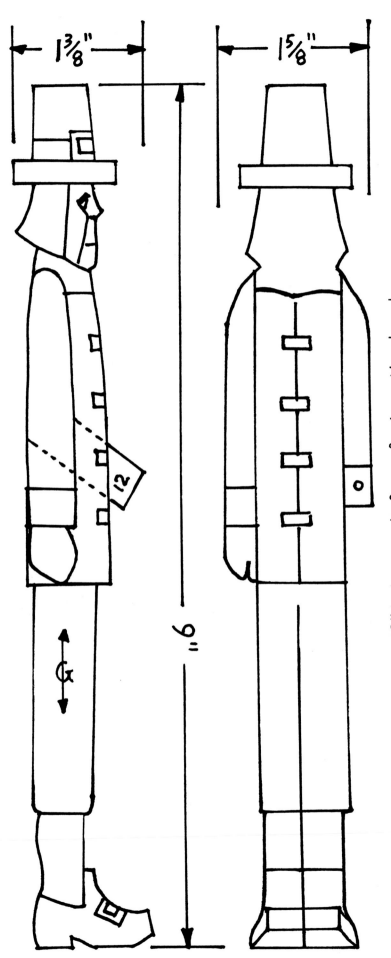

1³⁄₈"

1⁵⁄₈"

9"

12

Drill 1/8" hole in end of arm for inserting hand.

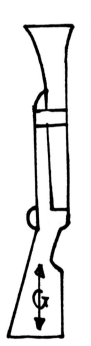

Rifle is sawn from a section of 3/8" thick wood.

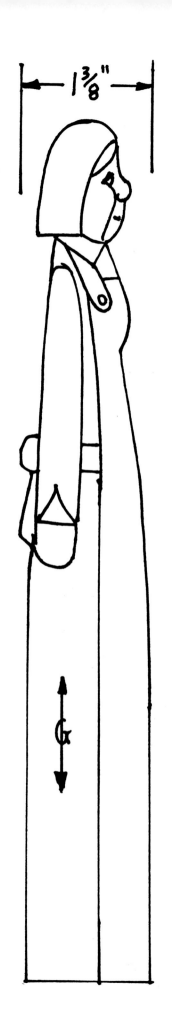

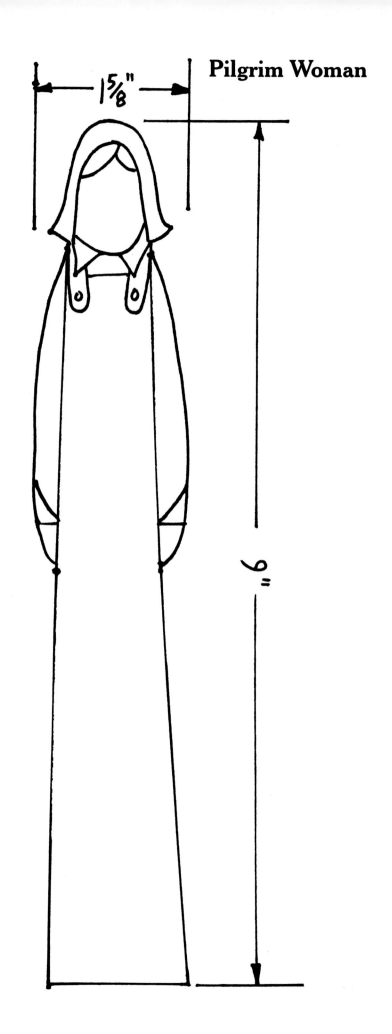

1 3/8"

1 5/8"

Pilgrim Woman

9"

G

Farmer Rabbit

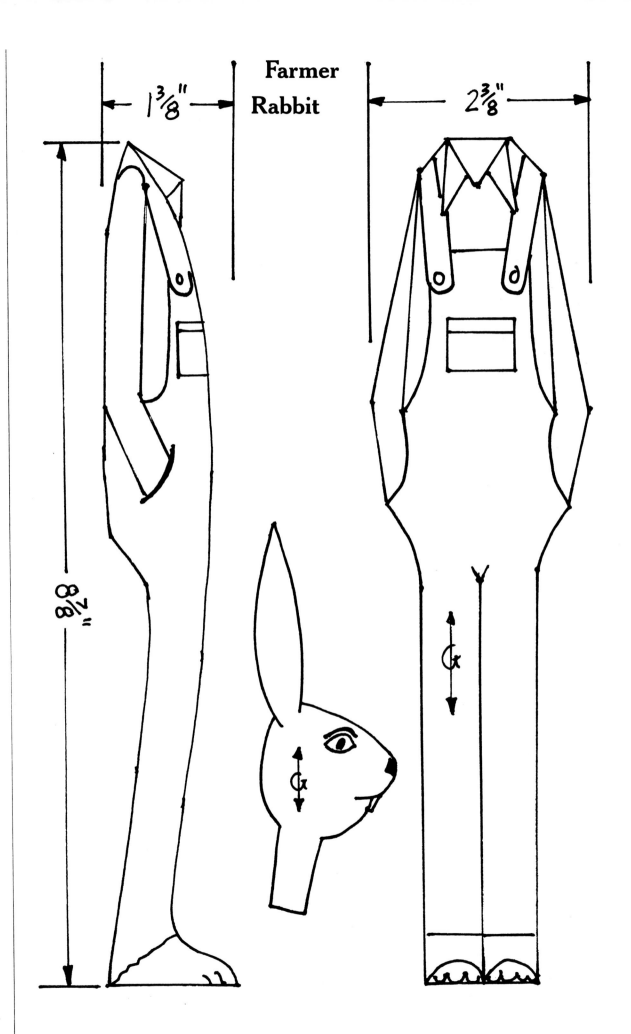

1⅜"

2⅜"

8½"

Gnome #2

$1\frac{3}{8}$"

6"

2"

Santa #4

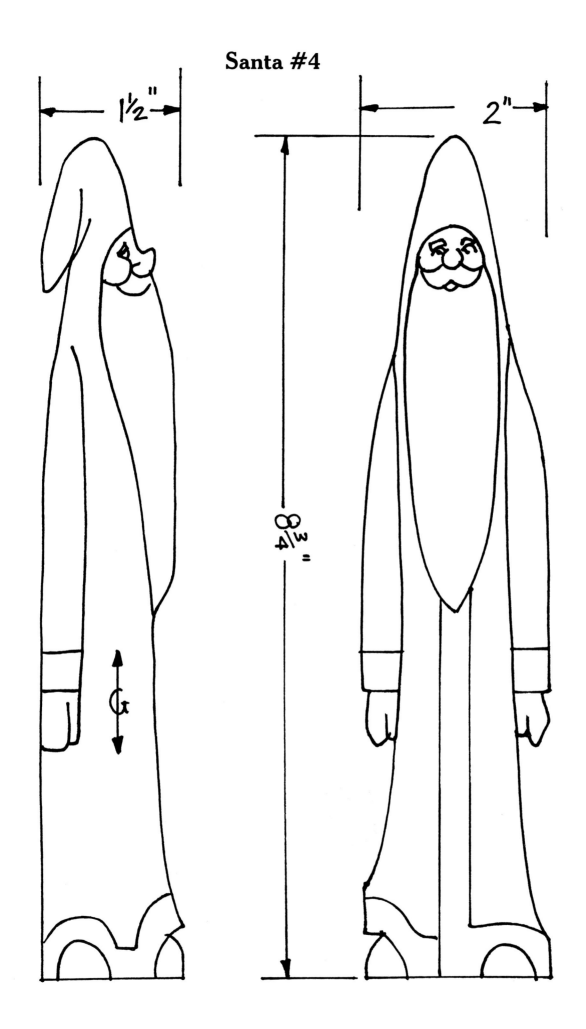

1½"

2"

8¾"

Cr

Uncle Sam #3

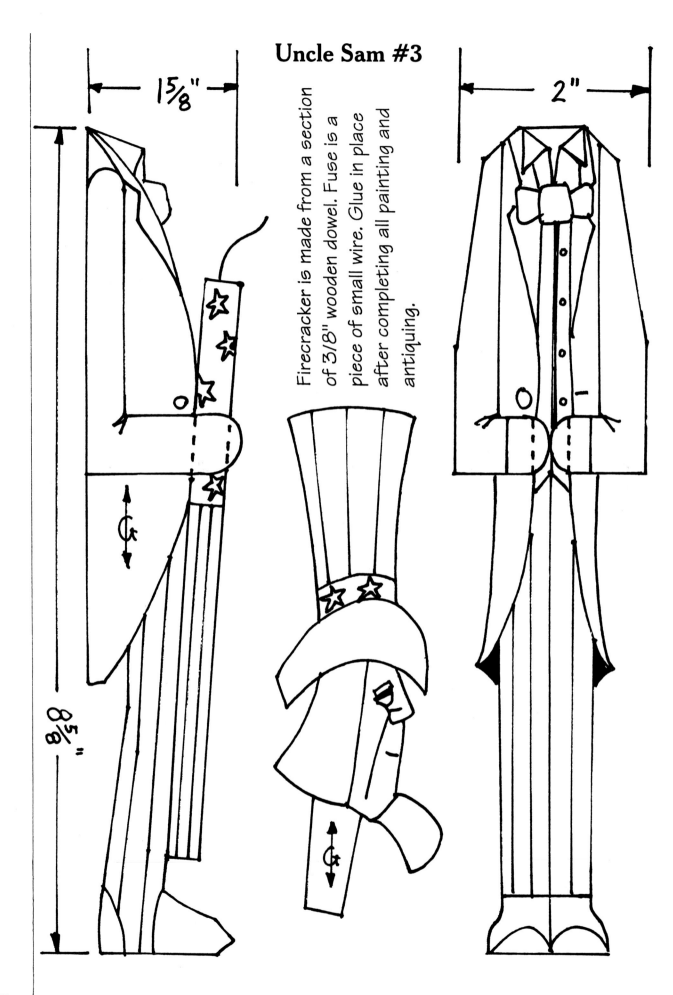

1⅝"

8⅝"

2"

Firecracker is made from a section of 3/8" wooden dowel. Fuse is a piece of small wire. Glue in place after completing all painting and antiquing.

Sea Captain

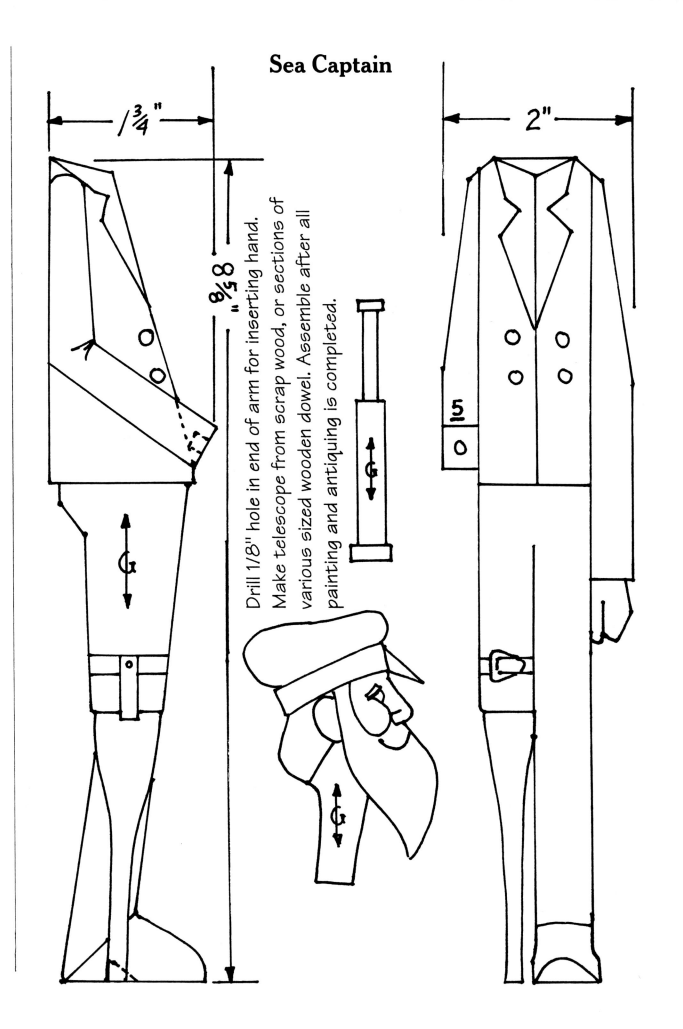

1 3/4"

8 5/8"

2"

Drill 1/8" hole in end of arm for inserting hand. Make telescope from scrap wood, or sections of various sized wooden dowel. Assemble after all painting and antiquing is completed.

Leprechaun #2

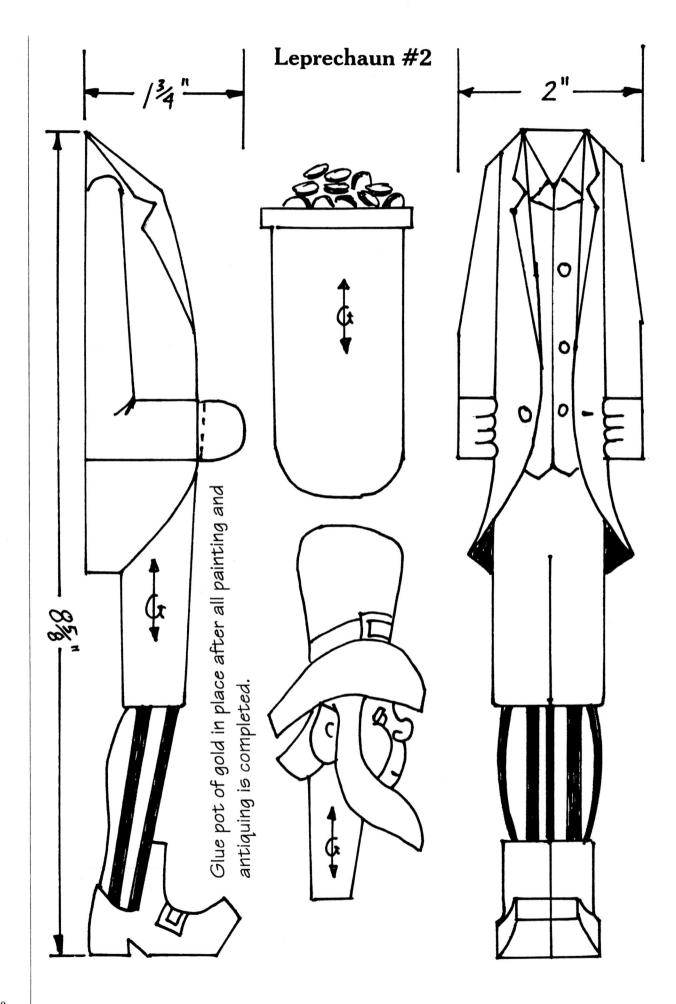

1¾"

2"

8⅝"

Glue pot of gold in place after all painting and antiquing is completed.

GOUGE REFERENCE CHART

(Reprinted with the permission of Woodcraft Supply Corp.)

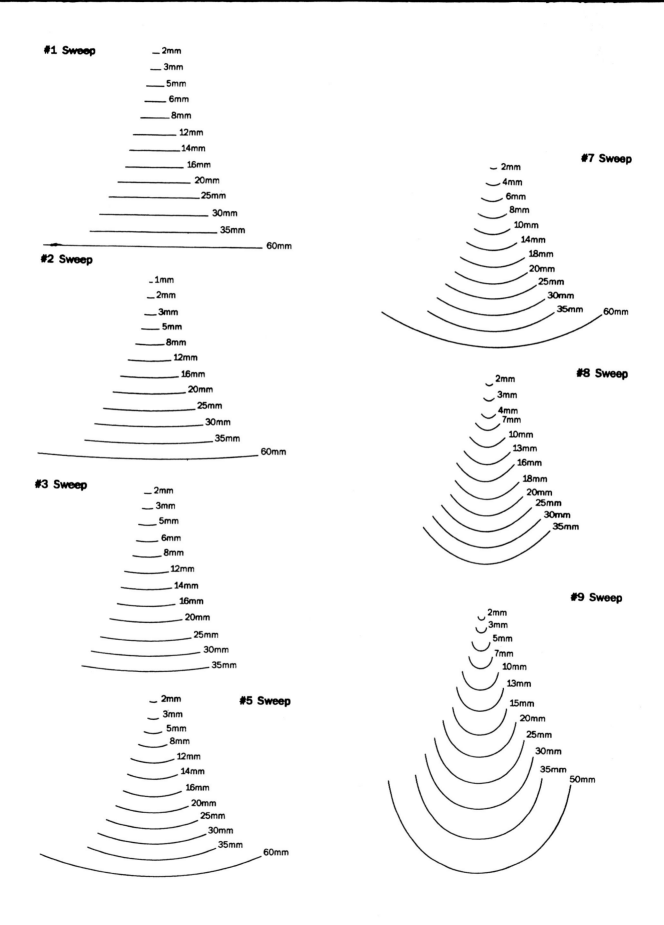

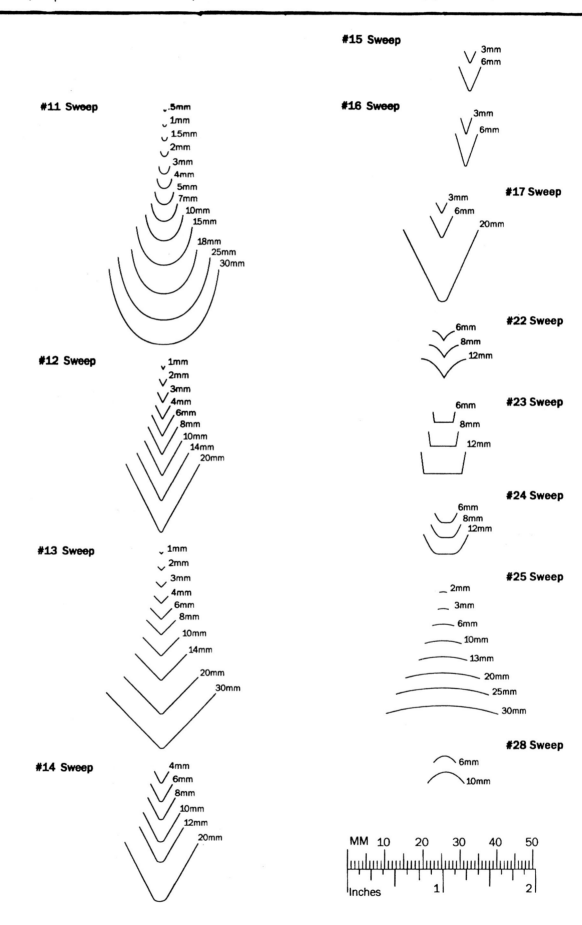

#11 Sweep
.5mm
1mm
1.5mm
2mm
3mm
4mm
5mm
7mm
10mm
15mm
18mm
25mm
30mm

#12 Sweep
1mm
2mm
3mm
4mm
6mm
8mm
10mm
14mm
20mm

#13 Sweep
1mm
2mm
3mm
4mm
6mm
8mm
10mm
14mm
20mm
30mm

#14 Sweep
4mm
6mm
8mm
10mm
12mm
20mm

#15 Sweep
3mm
6mm

#16 Sweep
3mm
6mm

#17 Sweep
3mm
6mm
20mm

#22 Sweep
6mm
8mm
12mm

#23 Sweep
6mm
8mm
12mm

#24 Sweep
6mm
8mm
12mm

#25 Sweep
2mm
3mm
6mm
10mm
13mm
20mm
25mm
30mm

#28 Sweep
6mm
10mm

MM 10 20 30 40 50
Inches 1 2

The Carving Project

For this project, we are going to carve a pirate with a cutlass in his hand and a parrot on his shoulder. (After all, how could he be an "official" pirate if he didn't have a parrot?) You will get practice carving accessories, and also in carving a caricature with a peg leg, if you've never carved one. We'll carve the head first, so we can capture the mood of the project. Then we'll carve a body for the head to sit on and a hand to hold the cutlass. Finally we'll carve the accessories, paint everything, then assemble the pieces and bring our project to life. Sharpen your knives and gouges, get comfortable, and let's get started!

Carving the Head

Draw lines to define the width of the neck. This width is not critical, but on this head I am making the neck about 1/2" wide.

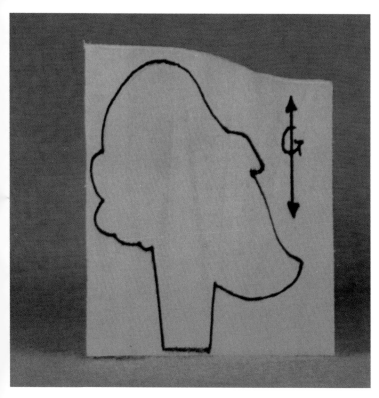

Transfer the head pattern to the wood and saw it out using a bandsaw, coping saw, or other means. Pay close attention to the direction of the wood grain in the photo. You want the grain to run vertically through the head. This will make carving easier and will give the head maximum strength.

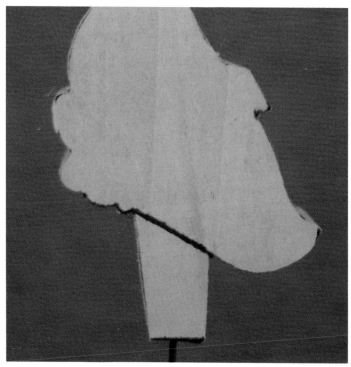

Also, sketch in a line on each side of the head to define the neck/beard separation.

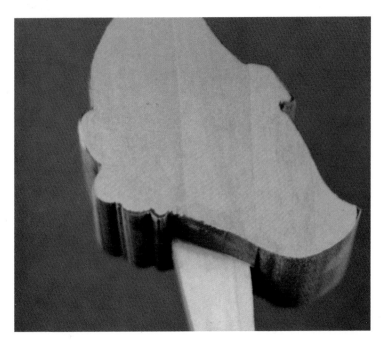

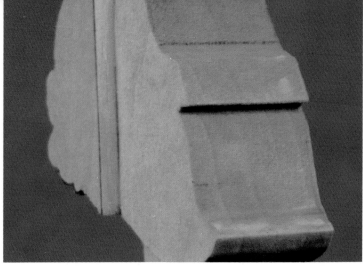

Incise these lines with your knife, and shave *toward* them from the *front* of the head, until about 1/4" of wood has been removed. This will narrow down the front section where the face is to be, and will make the ear section stand out from the head.

Using your knife, remove the excess wood from each side to establish the rough dimensions of the neck. We'll do more carving and shaping on the neck in a later step.

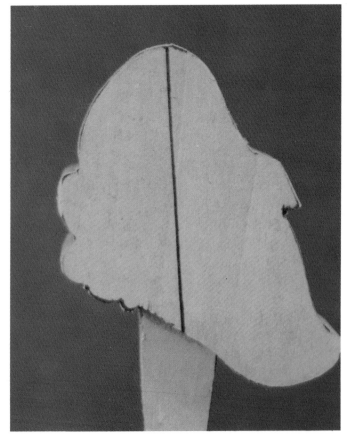

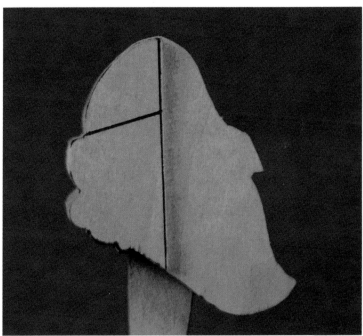

Sketch the scarf along the sides of the head. Incise the lines with your knife and shave **down** toward them from the **top** of the head, until this section is the same thickness as the front part of the head.

Now, sketch an ear on each side of the raised section. Incise around the ears with your knife, then remove all the wood from behind the ears by shaving *up* from the bottom and *in* from the rear of the head, until the head is a uniform thickness all around with just the ear sections protruding.

Sketch a line up each side of the head, to define the rear of the beard as well as the front of the ears. (This line should be slightly to the rear of the center of the head on the side).

34

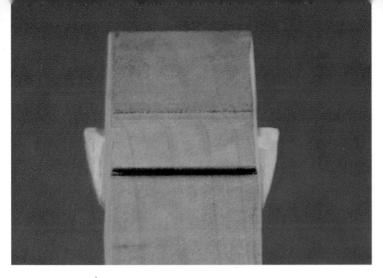

Using your knife, shave downward from the top of the ears to the bottom, so the ears taper to be flush with the face at the bottom. Let them rest now, and we'll do more detailing on them in a later step.

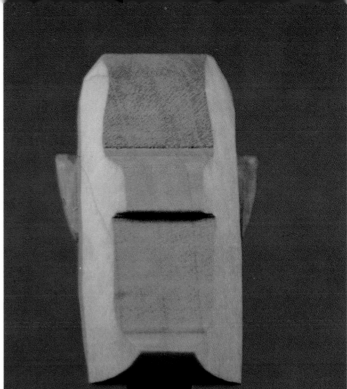

Now, use your knife and knock off all four sharp edges of the head at about a 45 degree angle, to begin the rough shaping and to make the carving a bit easier.

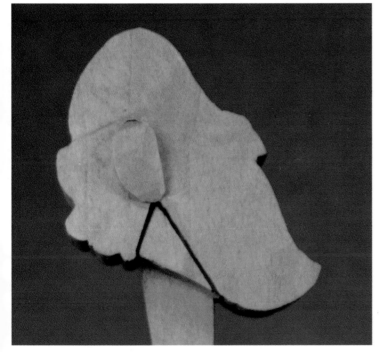

Draw an inverted "V" from the bottom of the ears to the front and rear edges of the neck, as shown.

Incise these lines with your knife, and remove the section of wood until you reach the level of the neck width you established earlier.

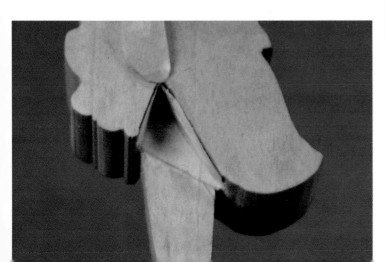

Sketch any parts of the scarf line that were carved away in the last step, and incise them about 1/16" deep with the tip of your knife. Using your knife, shave *upward* toward the scarf from below, so the scarf will stand out slightly from the head.

Now that we have the upper part of the scarf defined, go ahead and round off all the sharp edges on the upper half using your knife.

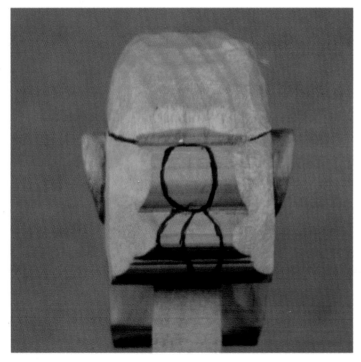

Next, sketch in the knot and scarf tails on the back of the head.

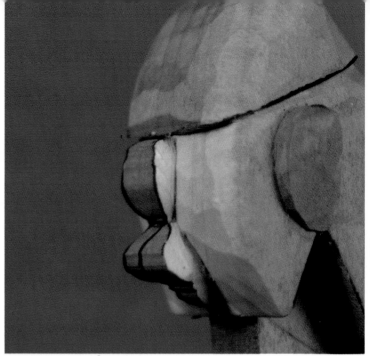

Incise these lines with the tip of your knife, then remove the excess wood from each side with your knife or an 8-millimeter #2 flat gouge, so the knot and tails stand out from the hair.

Incise the vertical line up the scarf tails to separate them, then remove a "V" shaped section of wood along this line to give the inner edges of the tails some definition.

Round off the sharp outer edges of the knot and scarf tails, and also the sharp edges of the hair on the back of the head.

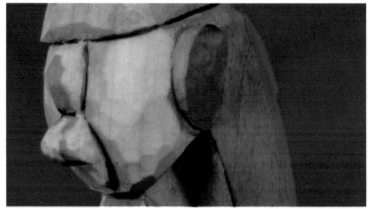

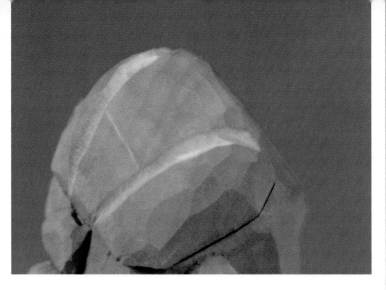

Sketch some wrinkle lines from the top front edge of the scarf down to the top of the knot in back . Go over these lines with a 1/4" "V" gouge to further define them and add a bit of detail to the scarf.

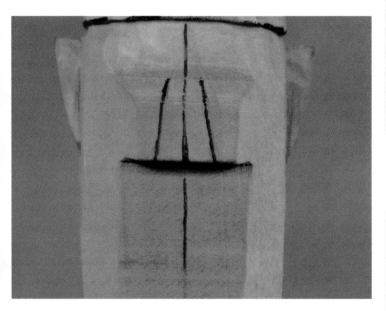

To begin detailing the face, first sketch in a centerline to help maintain symmetry, then sketch lines to define the width of the nose. Leave the nose a little on the wide side. (We can remove wood easier than trying to find a way to add wood back on).

Incise these lines using your knife, then remove the excess wood from each side so the rough shape of the nose is defined.

Clip off the bottom corners of the nose at about a 45-degree angle, then round off all the sharp edges.

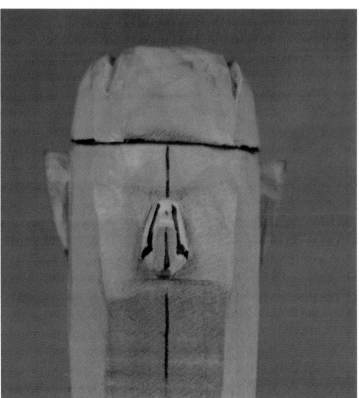

Mark the top of the nostril flare on the sides of the nose, and the narrower portion of the nose above the nostril flare.

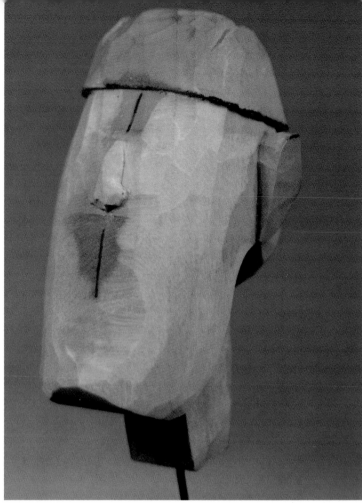

Incise these lines with your knife and remove the excess wood to give the nose a nice "Pirate" shape. Round off any new sharp edges this step produced.

Next, go over the entire front of the face and beard with your knife, removing any sharp edges.

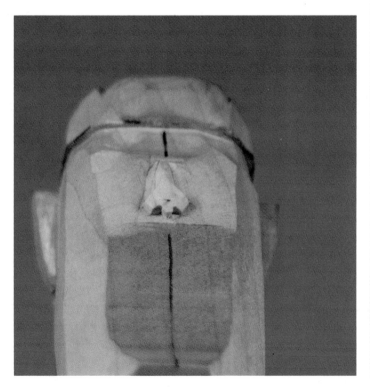

Remove two small "V"-shaped sections of wood from the bottom of the nose to simulate nostril openings.

Sketch in the eyepatch over the right eye, and draw the straps so they go over the tops of the ears and under the scarf (how convenient for us)!

Incise these lines about 1/16" deep with your knife tip, then shave toward them as appropriate to make the patch and strap stand out from the head.

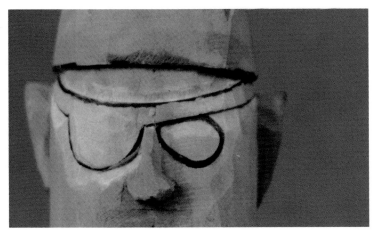

For the left eye, we'll use the mound method, as described in the "Tips" section of the book. First sketch in an oval shape, with the top slightly flattened, and incise the oval about 1/16" deep with the tip of your knife.

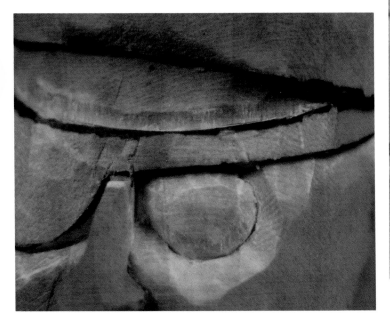

Shave toward the incision from both sides so the mound is separated from the face by a very small "V" channel.

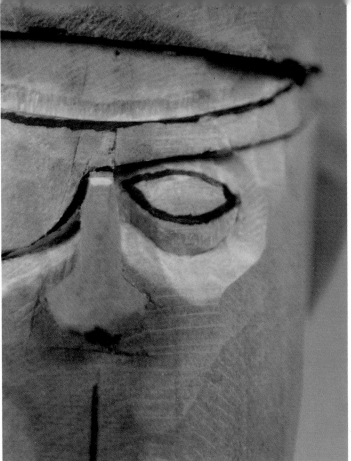

Divide the mound into thirds by sketching two curved, horizontal lines across it, making sure that the lines join at each corner of the mound.

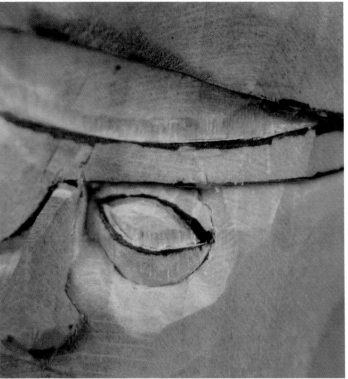

Using your knife tip, score each horizontal line about 1/16" deep. Working from the *center* of the eye mound, use your knife tip to shave *upward* toward the top horizontal line, and *downward* toward the bottom horizontal line. This will make the eyelids stand out from the eyeball area.

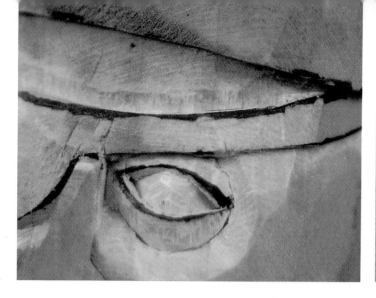

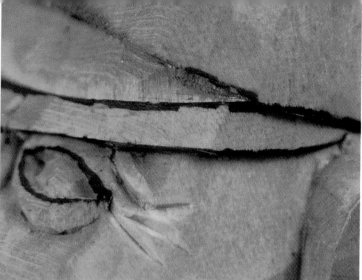

Finally, remove small triangular pieces of wood from the corners of the eye so the eyeball will be rounded from left to right, as well as top to bottom.

Add a few wrinkles at the corner of the eye, to help give the face a "weatherbeaten" look.

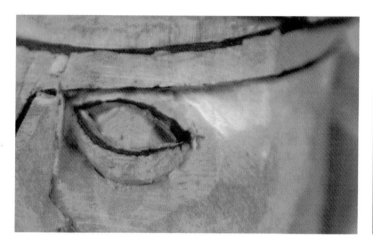

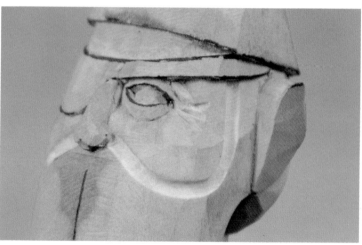

Using your knife, and with a curling motion, scoop away a small amount of wood slightly above the eye, *but below the strap*, to form an eyebrow over the left eye.

Sketch lines to define the beard, then use a #11 3-millimeter "U" gouge to follow the outlines of the beard, so the beard will be defined and separated from the face area. You may have to use your knife around the nose, and right below the eyepatch straps.

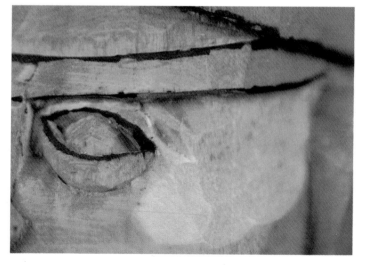

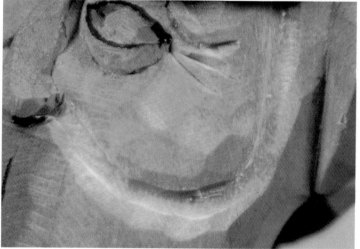

About even with the bottom of the eyes, shave away a small amount of wood all the way up to the bottom of the strap to define the cheek and temple area. Also, remove a small sliver of wood from the corner of the upper eyelid to add a bit more realism.

Use your knife to round off all the sharp edges of the cheeks and beard.

Sketch in a mustache shape, and separate it from the beard using a 1/4" "V" gouge, or your knife. Use your knife tip to remove a small triangle of wood at the bottom center of the mustache, then round off the sharp mustache and beard edges.

Remove the remaining sharp edges from the ears using your knife. Then, use a #11 3-millimeter "U" gouge to remove wood from the inside of the ears, cutting in from the rear edge of the ears toward the front of the head.

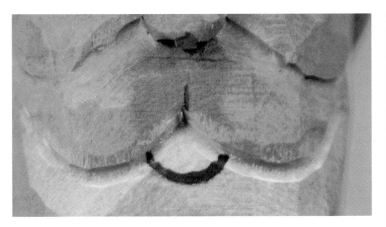

Sketch in a small semi-circle to represent the lower lip, and incise the line about 1/16" deep with your detail knife tip.

Use a #11 2-millimeter "U" or 1/8" "V" gouge to put detail into the hair and beard.

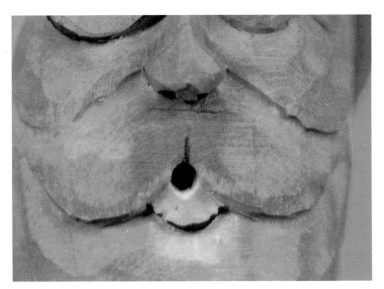

Use your knife to shave away a small amount of wood below the lip line, so the lip will stand out from the beard. Next, using a small nailset or small drill bit (a 1/8" bit seems to be about the right size), make a mouth hole.

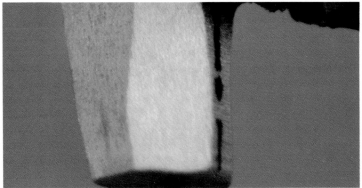

Use your knife to remove the sharp edges from the two *front* edges of the neck. This will start the process of rounding the neck.

Now, remove the sharp corners from the *rear* edges of the neck. Then go all around the neck, removing sharp edges, until you have a round neck. The size of the neck you end with will determine how big a hole you will drill in the body later to receive it.

At this point, we are through with the head and face carving. Look it over, and clean up any areas that don't appeal to you. Now, we need to make a body for the head to sit on.

Carving the Body

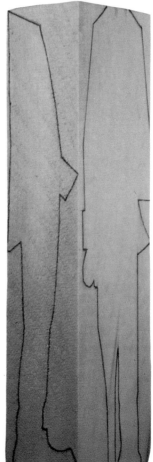

Transfer the side and front views of the body pattern to a block of wood. Note the grain direction runs *vertically* from the feet to the shoulders. If you wish to drill the neck hole at this time, refer back to the "Tips" section for the procedure. For this project, we will drill it in a later step.

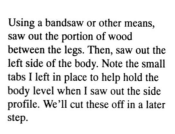

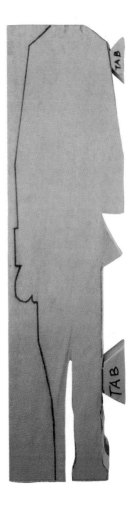

Using a bandsaw or other means, saw out the portion of wood between the legs. Then, saw out the left side of the body. Note the small tabs I left in place to help hold the body level when I saw out the side profile. We'll cut these off in a later step.

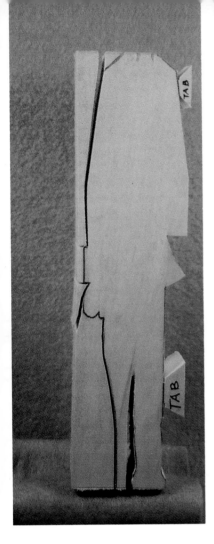  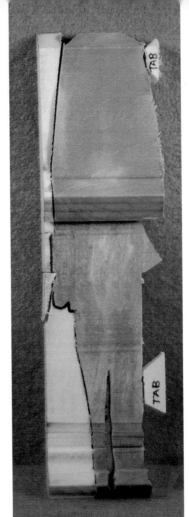 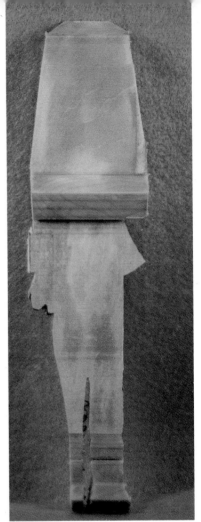

As you can see here, I have made a series of saw cuts on the right side of the body, but I haven't actually removed any of the wood. These will serve as references so I will know where to remove wood later, after I saw out the side profile.

Now sketch the lines back in on the right side of the front view, using the reference cuts you made earlier as a guide.

Turn the wood on its edge, and saw out the side view. Here is where the tabs are handy in helping keep the wood level.

Finish sawing out the right side of the body, and also saw off the tabs at this time.

To make a hole in the collar for the neck, use a drill bit that is slightly larger than the neck you carved and drill a hole straight down into the body, about 1/2" deep. You may want to clamp the body in a vise while you do this.

Trim and taper the neck as needed, to make a snug fit in the neck hole when viewed from the side. Use your knife to adjust the length of the neck so the head rests against the top of the body.

A view from the side.

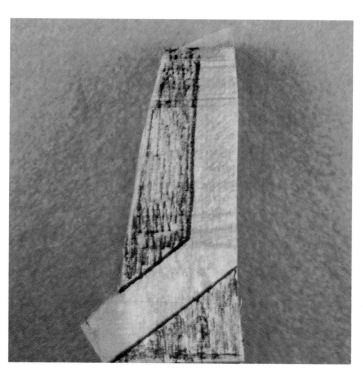

Sketch in the left arm. Remove the darkened sections of wood to a depth of about 3/8" using your knife or an 8-millimeter #2 flat gouge.

And from the front.

Remove the excess wood from the front of the body to flatten the chest area and make the left arm stand out, using your knife or 8-millimeter #2 flat gouge.

Sketch the cuff on the left sleeve. Use your knife or 1/8" "V" gouge to make a small "V" channel to separate the cuff from the sleeve, following the line you sketched. Also cut a few wrinkles in the crook of the elbow, using your knife.

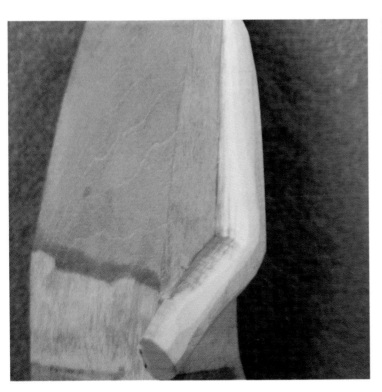

Round off all the sharp edges on the left arm and shoulder.

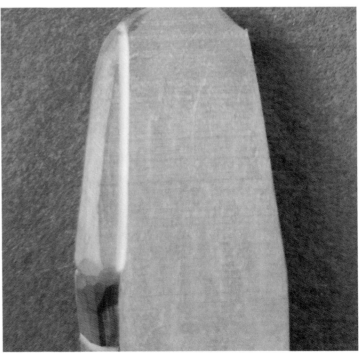

Mark the back of the left arm. Use your knife or a 1/8" "V" gouge to cut a small "V" channel up the back and over the shoulder until the left arm is well-defined.

Finally, drill a 1/8" hole, about 1/4" deep into the end of the left arm to insert the hand in later.

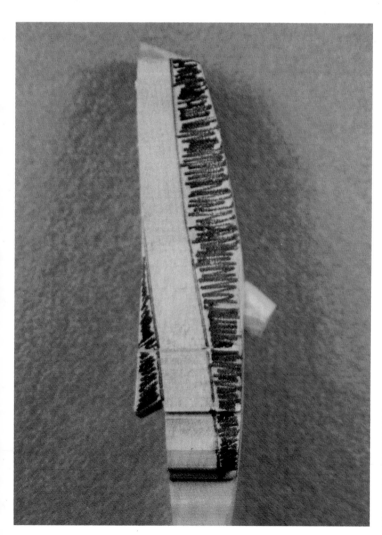

Sketch in the right arm and hand.

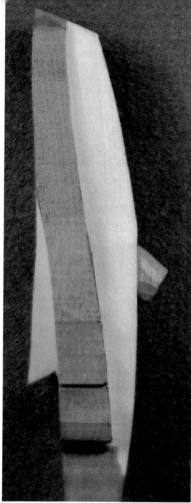

Using your knife or an 8-millimeter #2 flat gouge, remove the darkened sections of wood as you did on the left arm earlier.

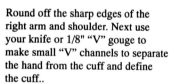

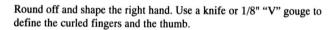

Round off the sharp edges of the right arm and shoulder. Next use your knife or 1/8" "V" gouge to make small "V" channels to separate the hand from the cuff and define the cuff..

Round off and shape the right hand. Use a knife or 1/8" "V" gouge to define the curled fingers and the thumb.

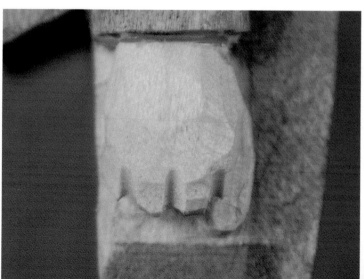

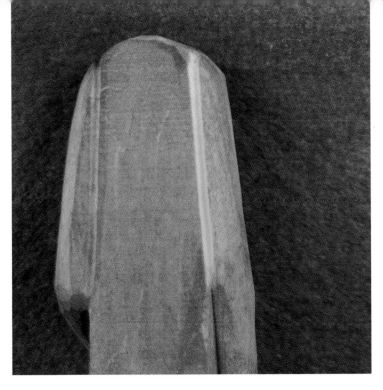 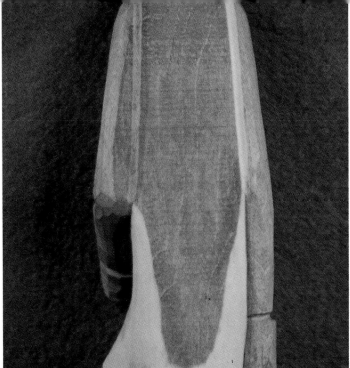

Mark the back of the right arm as you did earlier for the left arm. Use your knife or a 1/8" "V" gouge to cut a small "V" channel up the back and over the shoulder so the right arm will be well-defined.

And in back. Round off any new sharp edges this last procedure created. (We'll round off and shape the lower part of the body later in the project).

 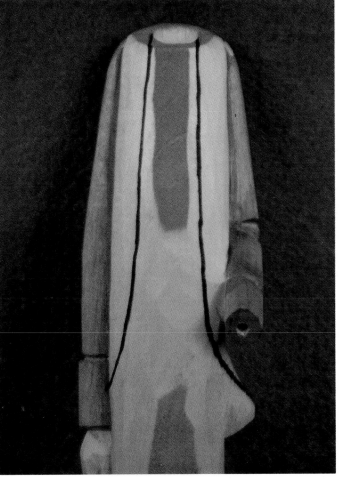

Starting at a point about even with the bottom of the right hand, use your knife to remove the sharp edges from the body in front.

Draw the coat in front.

Draw the coat down around the left side. Incise these lines with your knife about 1/8" deep.

Sketch in the lapels of the coat up the front, and around the back of the coat. Incise these lines using your knife tip, then shave toward them working from the outer edges of the coat, so the lapels and collar will stand out slightly.

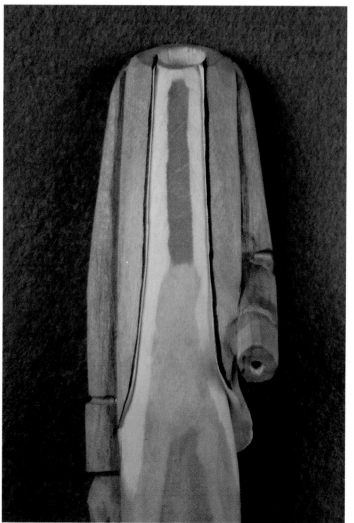

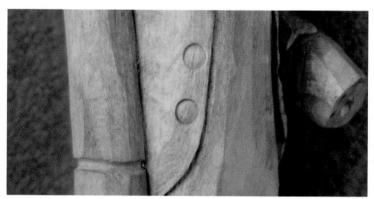

Add buttons to the right side of the coat using a small nailset or eye punch, and use a 1/8" "V" gouge to make buttonholes on the left side of the coat.

Shave back toward these lines, working from the center of the chest outward and from the legs upward until the wood comes free. This will give the coat some definition, and make it stand out from the body. On the sides, you may need to take off a little more wood so the coat will stand out from the legs.

Sketch in the belt and buckle. Incise the lines with your knife, and shave toward them as appropriate, removing small amounts of wood.

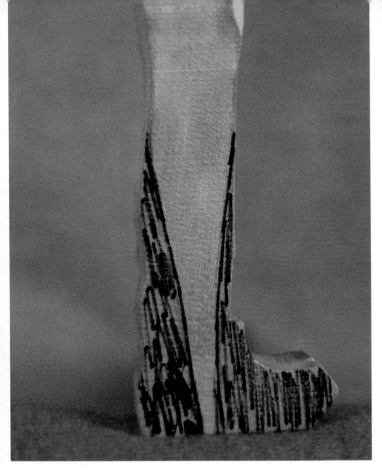

Sketch in the side view of the peg leg. Try to make the side view taper about the same as that in the front view (which has already been shaped by the saw). Then remove the darkened areas of wood using your knife...

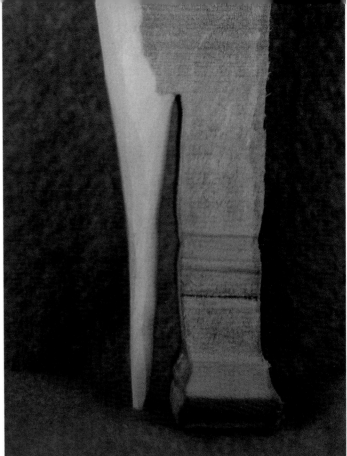

....use your knife to knock off all four sharp edges on the peg leg, then remove the new sharp edges produced, until the right leg and peg are fairly round.

To obtain this shape....

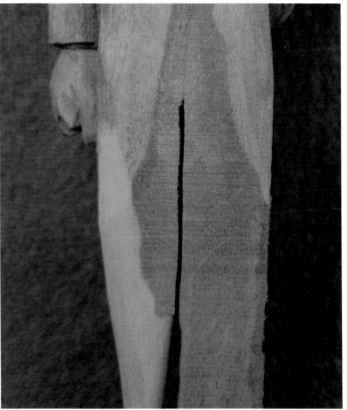

Sketch a center line up the legs in front and back.

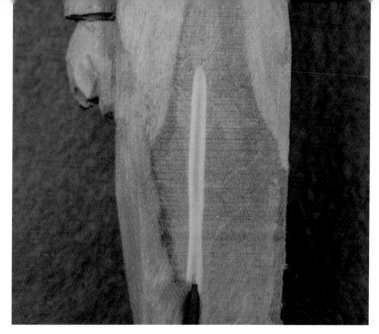

Go over these lines with your knife tip or 1/8" "V" gouge to make a "V" channel and define the leg separation.

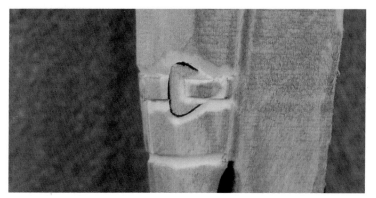

Sketch the line around the top of the peg leg, and sketch in the straps and buckle. (Pay close attention to the strap as shown on the pattern front and side views). Incise these lines about 1/16" deep with your knife tip and shave toward them as appropriate so they will stand out from the pant leg.

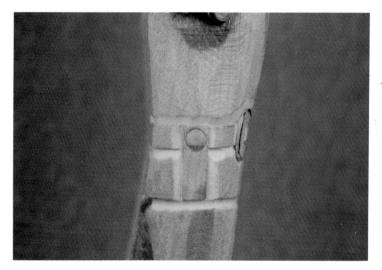

Use a 1/8" eye punch to make the small button on the vertical strap.

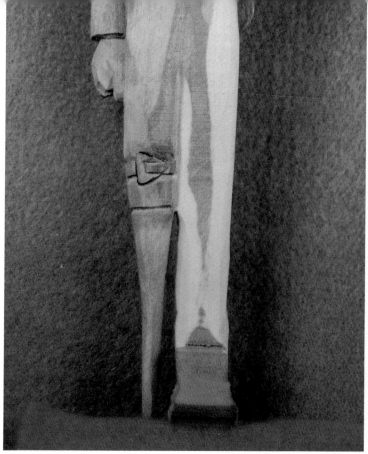

Use your knife to round and shape the left leg (trouser and stocking) the same way as you rounded the arms previously.

Sketch a line around the bottom of the left trouser leg. Follow this line with a 1/4" "V" gouge to separate the trouser leg from the stocking. Then shave upward lightly with your knife to blend the stocking into the bottom of the trouser.

50

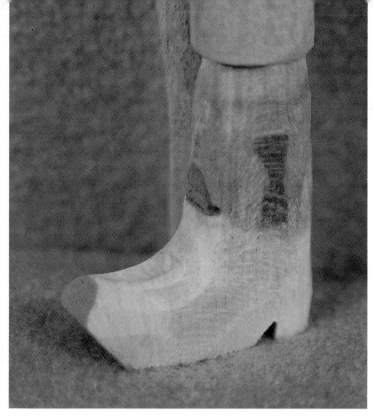

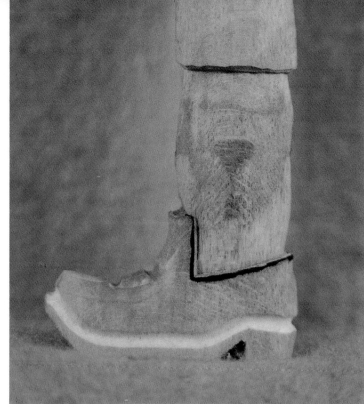

Round off all the sharp edges on the upper part of the shoe, all the way around, using your knife.

Using a 1/8" "V" gouge, go around the lower edge of the shoe to define the sole, and separate it from the upper part of the shoe. This completes the body carving. Let's move on so we can get the left hand, parrot, and cutlass carved. You're doing fine so far. Stay with me and soon we'll have a complete pirate!

Carving the Hand

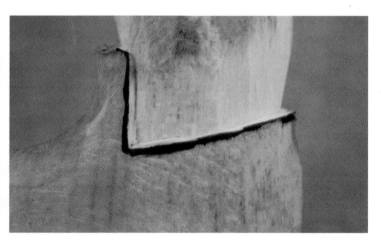

Sketch in some lines to define the shoe and stocking separation. Incise these lines about 1/16" deep with your knife. Shave down from the stocking toward the top of the shoe so a small amount of wood is removed. This will give the illusion of the leg going into the shoe.

Next, sketch a buckle on the top of the shoe. Go around the outside lines of the buckle using a 1/8" "V" gouge. Remove a small portion of wood from the inside of the buckle using your knife tip, or a 3-millimeter #11 "U" gouge.

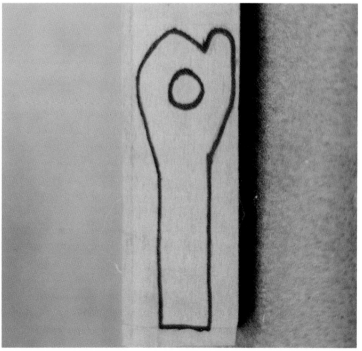

Lay out the top view of the hand on a piece of 3/4" thick basswood. Also, sketch in a circle to indicate where we will drill a hole in the next step. Notice I have drawn a short section of wood attached to the rear of the hand. This section will serve as a handle while I carve and shape the hand and will form the wrist peg in a later step.

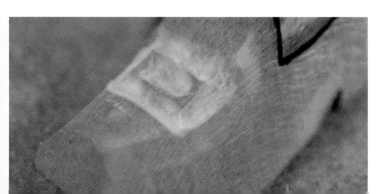

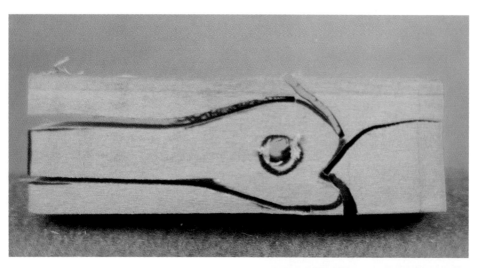

Drill a 3/16" hole down through the hand, then partially saw out the top profile of the hand. If you drill the hole before sawing, you lessen the chance of splitting the wood.

Use your knife and round off all the sharp edges of the hand. Next, sketch in the thumb and finger section.

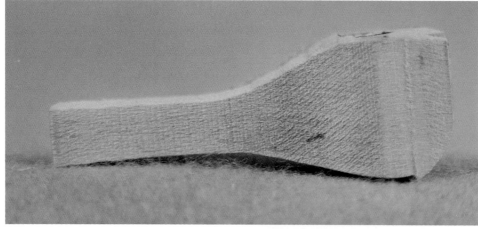

Remove wood from the hand using your knife so the thumb and finger section is well-defined. Then round off the sharp edges of the thumb and finger section.

Using the top set of hands in "Hand Studies" as a reference, sketch in the side profile of the hand and saw it out. Then finish sawing out the top profile. You should now have a hand that will require very little work to finish.

Draw a line in the middle of the finger section to divide it in half, then draw lines to divide each of these sections in half. You should now have four fingers defined, all approximately equal.

Using a 1/8" "V" gouge, go over these lines so the fingers will be separated. At this point, if you do nothing else you have a hand that will look perfectly good once it is painted. More experienced carvers may add more detailing as desired, such as knuckles and wrinkles on the finger joints.

Using your knife, trim the section of wood down to form a "wrist" that will fit snugly into the hole you drilled earlier in the left arm. When done properly, the hand should appear to be coming out of the sleeve. This method allows you to turn the hands in various directions, so your carvings will appear more lifelike. Also, use your knife to round off any remaining sharp edges until the hand is fairly smooth all over. You may glue the hand in place now or wait until it is painted, whatever is easier for you.

Carving the Cutlass

Turn the wood on its side and mark a section that is approximately 5/8" wide, the length of the cutlass. Saw away the darkened wood.

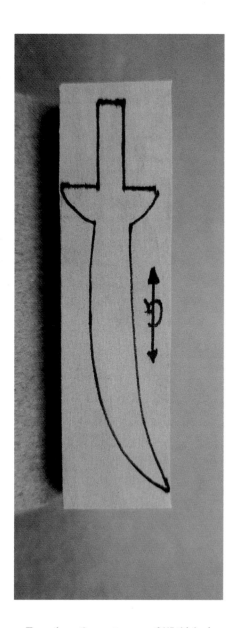

Trace the cutlass pattern on a 3/4" thick piece of basswood. Saw it out with a bandsaw or coping saw. Pay close attention to the indicated grain direction.

Now mark a 1/4" wide section along the center of the cutlass blade and cutlass handle. Saw away the darkened wood, but do not reduce the width of the hand guard.

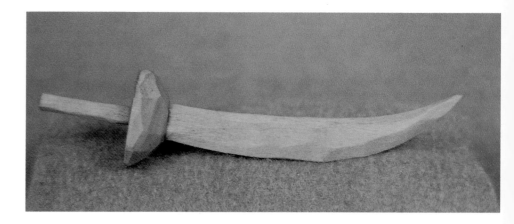

Now, using your knowledge of rounding square areas, use your knife to round off the blade, hand guard, and handle. The handle is round enough when it will fit in the hole you drilled in the hand earlier.

Carving the Parrot

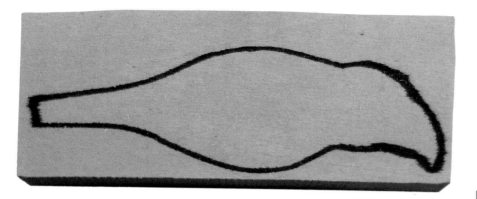

Trace the side view of the parrot on a section of 3/4" thick wood and saw it out. The grain runs lengthwise along the body.

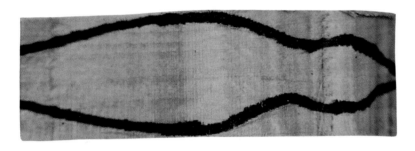

Now sketch in the top profile of the parrot as shown and saw it out.

Finally, mark an eye on each side of the head, and use a 1/8" eyepunch to give it detail. At this point, we are through with the carving steps. I am going to go ahead and make a base for the pirate now so I can paint everything in one sitting. I used a piece of wood 2" x 2" square, by 1-1/2" thick for the base. Since the pencil people are so tall in relation to their width, it is almost a necessity to mount them on bases for stability.

Round off all the sharp edges using your knife, then sketch in the lines of the beak. Incise with your knife, then shave toward the lines until a small amount of wood is removed.

Next, sketch in the wing lines on the sides. Incise the lines with your knife and shave up toward them from the bottom of the parrot. This will make the wings stand out slightly.

Painting and Assembling the Project

Paint the face, lip, ears, neck, and hands with fleshtone.

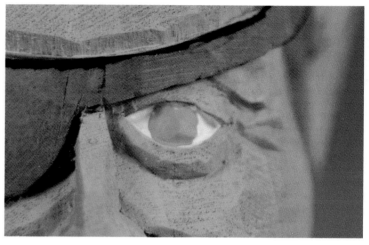

Now take a small, fine-tip brush and put a round dot of Blue Heaven in the center of the eye.

When this is dry, use your fine-tip brush to put a black dot inside the blue dot. The placement of the blue and black dots will have various effects on the facial expression. Experiment on a piece of scrap wood to discover all the expressions you can create. I personally like to show the eyes rolled upward, looking toward one side or the other. You may experiment with different looks and find one that you prefer also.

Paint the eyeball white.

Finally, take a toothpick and put a white highlight on the edge of the black dot. If the eyes are looking to the left, I put the highlight around the 10-o'clock position. If looking to the right, I put the highlight around the 2-o'clock position. When looking straight ahead, as the eye is here, you can put the highlight at either the 10-o'clock or 2-o'clock position, whichever you prefer. This is another area you can experiment with on a scrap piece of wood to see the effects of moving the highlight around.

The scarf is painted crimson and the eyepatch and straps are painted black.

The beard, hair, and eyebrow are painted dark brown. When this is dry, use a dry brush dipped in Quaker Grey to lightly go over the high spots of the beard and hair to add a few highlights.

Paint the coat navy blue with Kim Gold buttons. The shirt is painted with alternating stripes of antique white and crimson.

The belt is black with a silver buckle, and the trousers are Trail Tan.

The stocking on the left leg is Ocean Reef Blue, and the shoe is painted Brown Iron Oxide with a Kim Gold buckle.

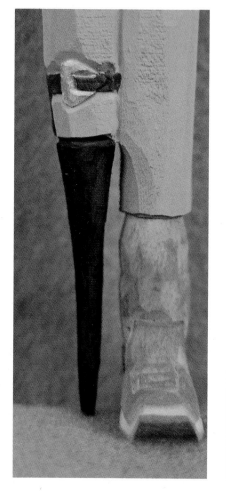

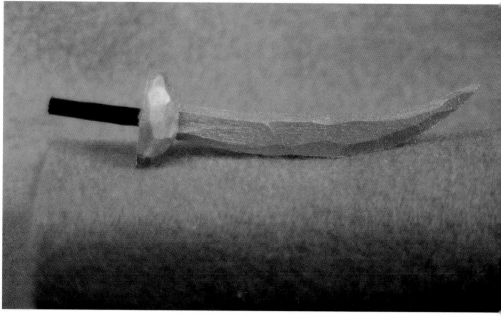

Paint the pegleg walnut with burnt sienna straps. The buckle and button on the strap are silver.

Paint the cutlass blade and hand guard silver. The handle is black.

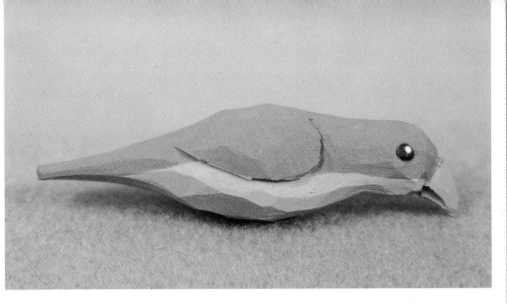

The belly and lower areas of the parrot are painted bright yellow, and the upper area is vibrant green. The beak is Cadet Grey, and the eyes are black with a tiny white highlight.

If you wish to antique and varnish the pieces, now is the time to do so. Refer to the section on "Antiquing" for more information.

Put a drop of glue in the hole in the left hand. Insert the cutlass handle into it until the hand guard seats against the hand. Then glue the hand into the left arm.

When everything is dry, put a drop of glue on the bottom of the neck and insert it into the hole you drilled in the body earlier. I like to have the head turned slightly to one side, as I believe it makes the carving look less stiff.

Insert a straight pin down into the top of the right shoulder. Cut it off so about 1/4" is left protruding above the shoulder. Put a drop of glue on the pin and press the parrot down onto the pin until the belly of the bird sits flush with the wood. The pin will support the parrot until the glue dries, and will add strength to this area.

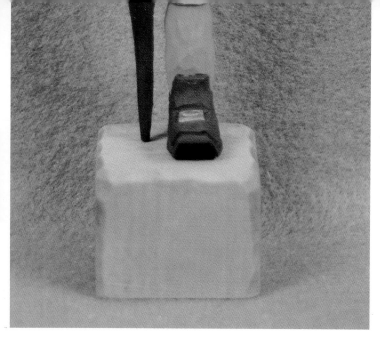

Put glue on the bottom of the shoe and pegleg, and mount the pirate to his base. (NOTE: Paint or stain the base a color of your choice before gluing the pirate to it.)

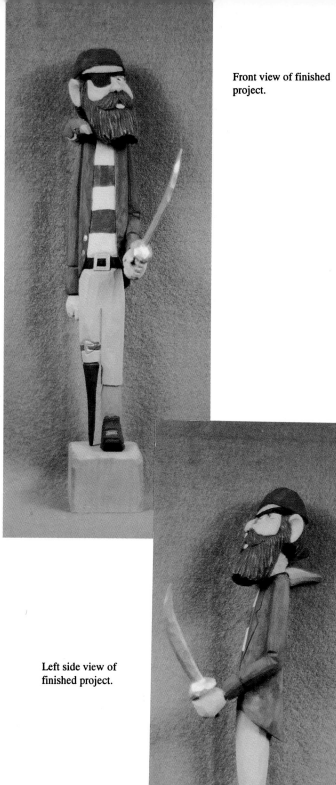

Front view of finished project.

Right side view of finished project.

Left side view of finished project.

Antiquing the Project

Once the paint is dry, you may want to "age" your carvings with an antiquing product in order to help tone down the colors a bit. I have had excellent results using antiquing gels made by Delta Technical coatings. These are available at hobby and craft stores. They come in various colors so you can create different effects.

Brush a coat of antiquing gel on the carving, then wipe it off using a damp rag or sponge. It is your option how much you wipe off. After the antiquing is dry, I like to finish my carvings with a coat of brush-on acrylic varnish. Delta Technical Coatings also makes an excellent varnish. I prefer the one that leaves a satin finish. This particular finish is not too flat nor too glossy, but leaves a "soft" look to the completed carving. **(I usually put a coat of varnish on the face, hands, and hair area *before* I antique the carving.)** This will prevent these areas from absorbing too much antiquing color.

A Final Note

That's it! We're through for now. Sit back, take a rest, and admire your new creation. I hope you enjoyed this project as much as I did. Until next time ... good carving, and please keep those letters and phone calls coming. I really do appreciate hearing from all of you!

I hope that in some way I have been able to help each of you with some aspect of carving and painting. When we share tips and information, we all become better. If you have any comments or questions about something in this book, or if you have an idea you'd like to see me put in a future book, please feel free to write or call me at the following address and telephone number. I welcome any comments or suggestions you have.

Al Streetman
1609 N. Fordson Drive
Oklahoma City, Ok. 73127
(405) 495-0816

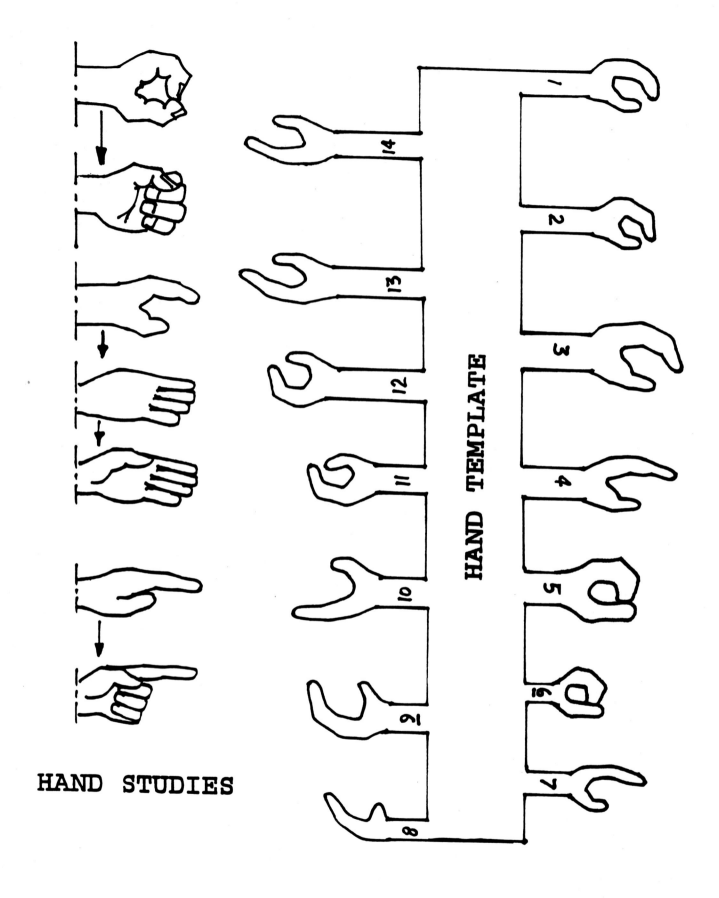

HAND STUDIES

HAND TEMPLATE

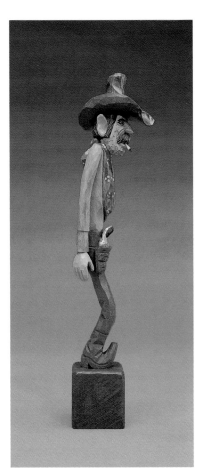
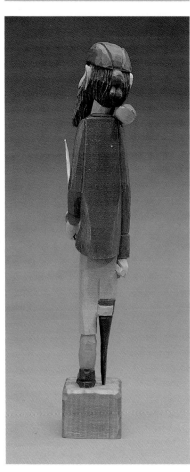

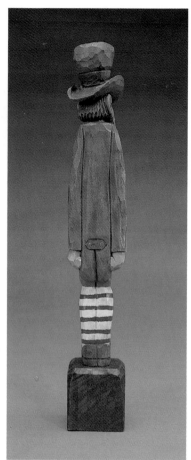